ART THERAPY COLORING

FLOWER
COLORING BOOK
FOR ADULTS VOL 5

Preview of Coloring Pages

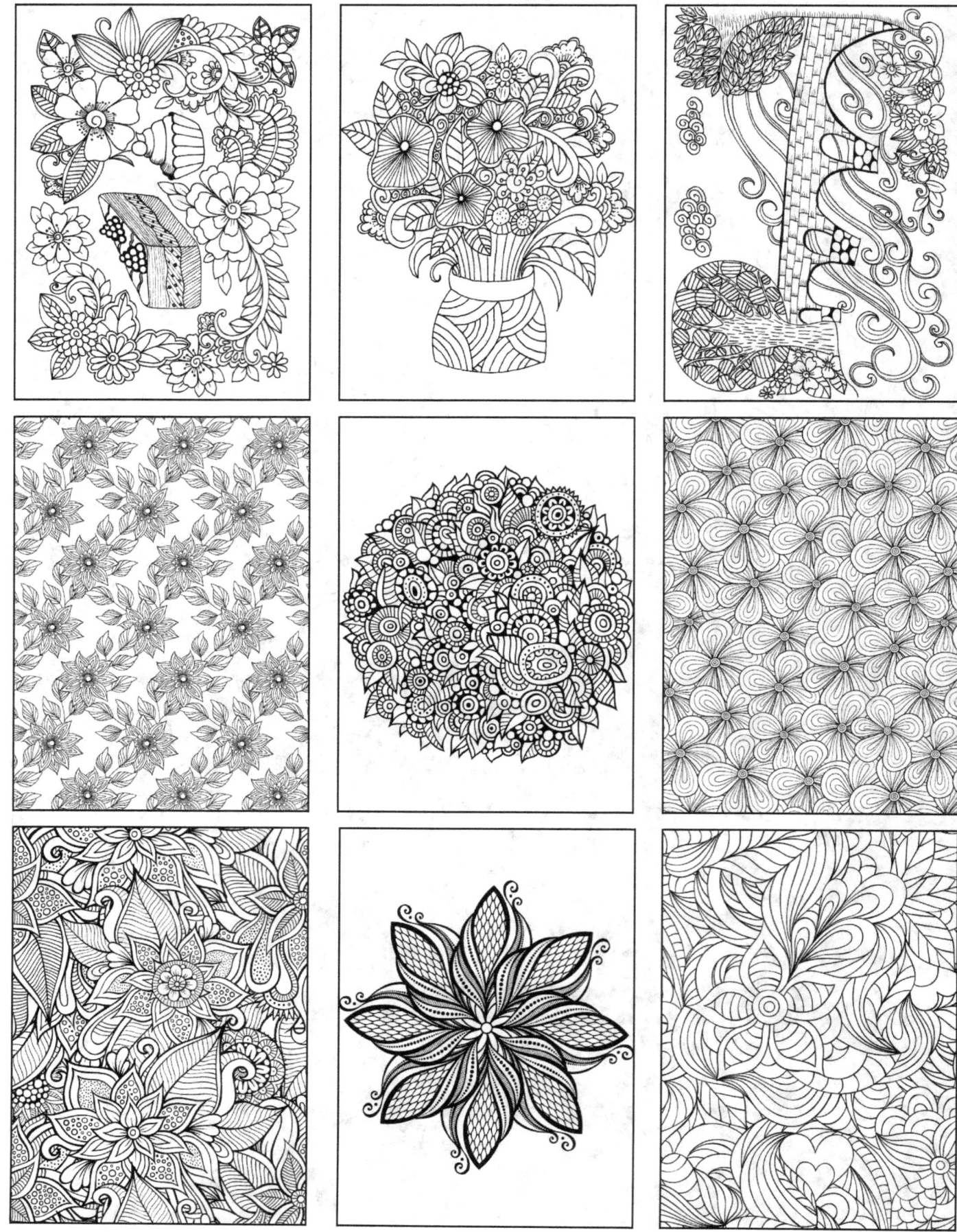

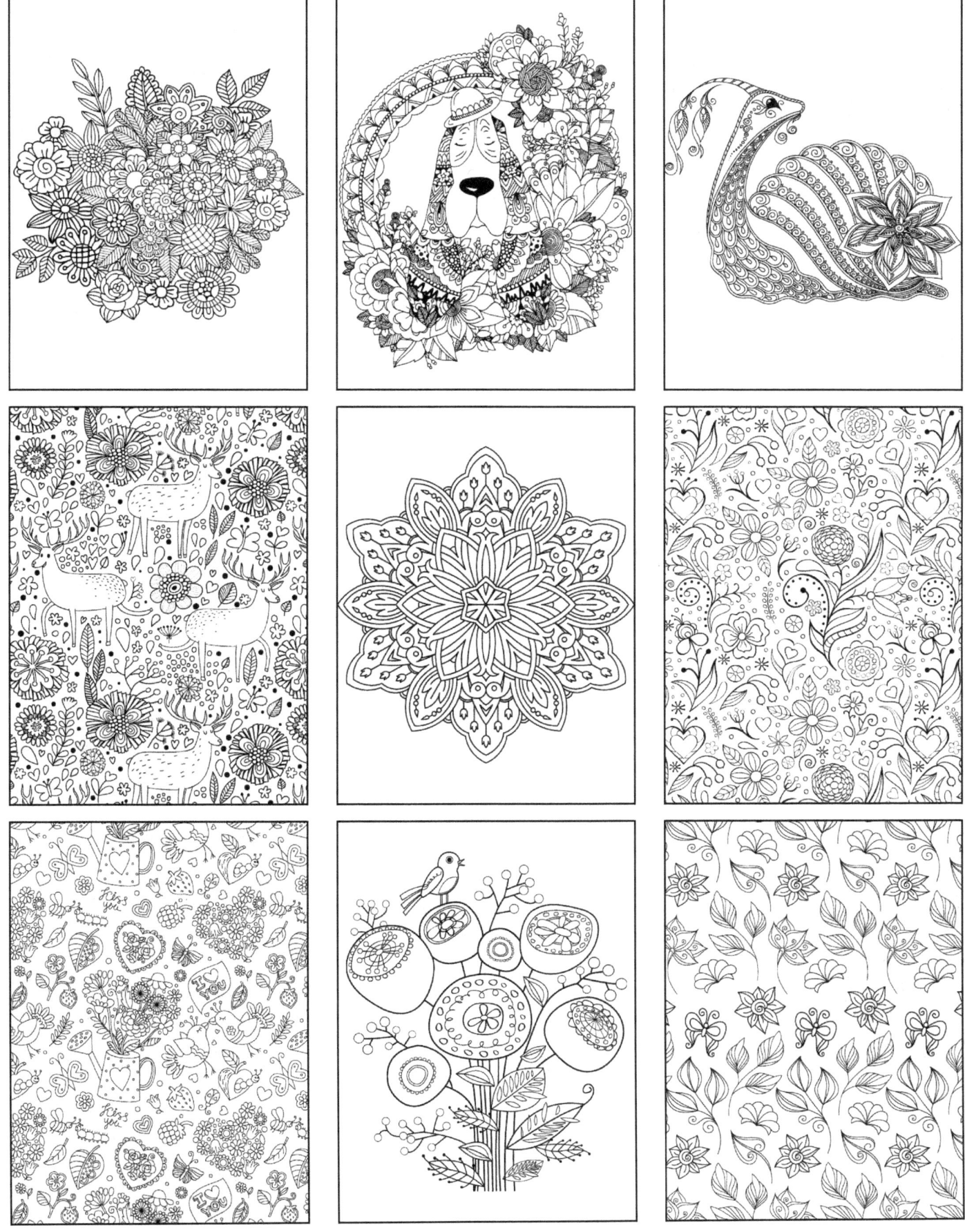

Preview of Coloring Pages

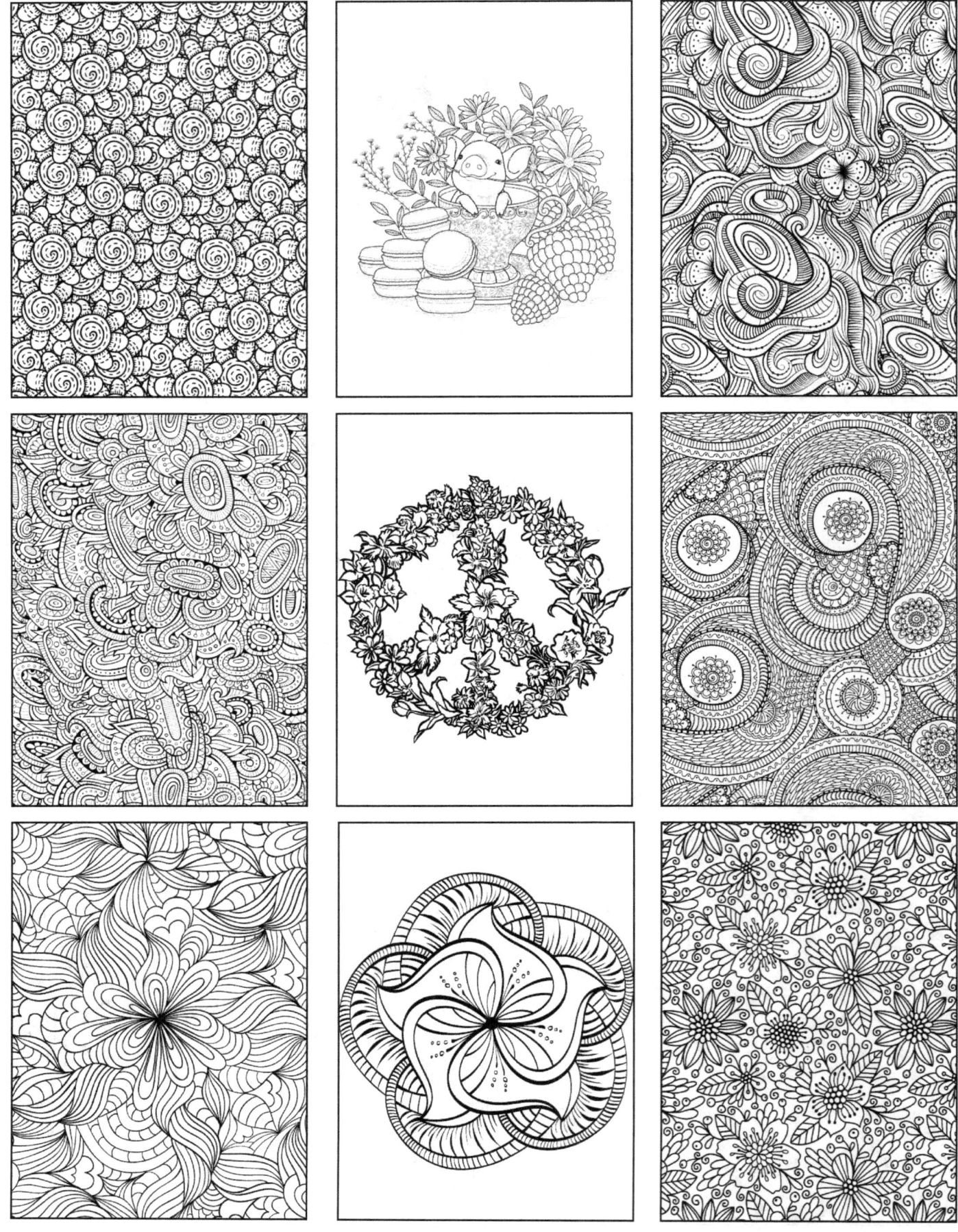

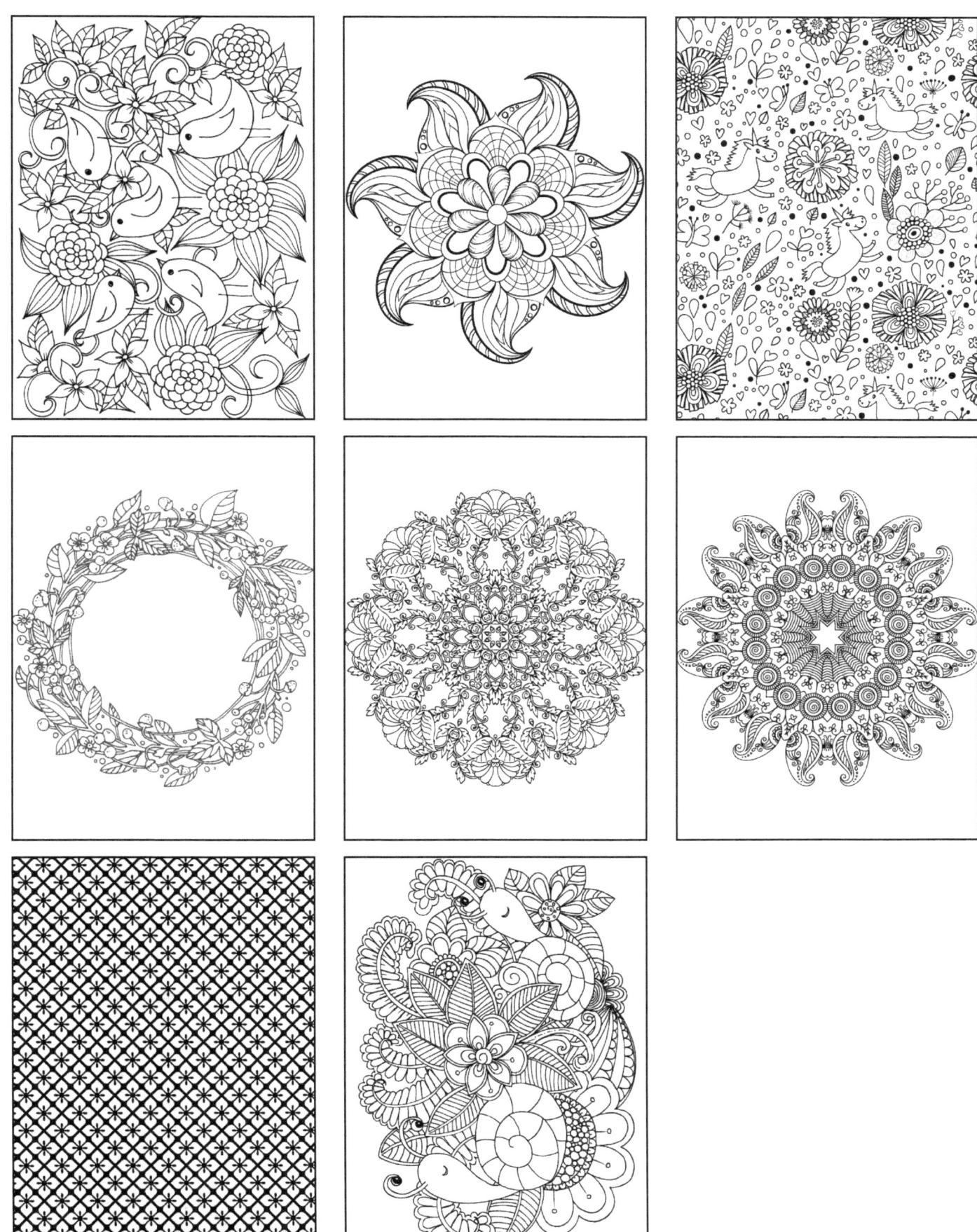

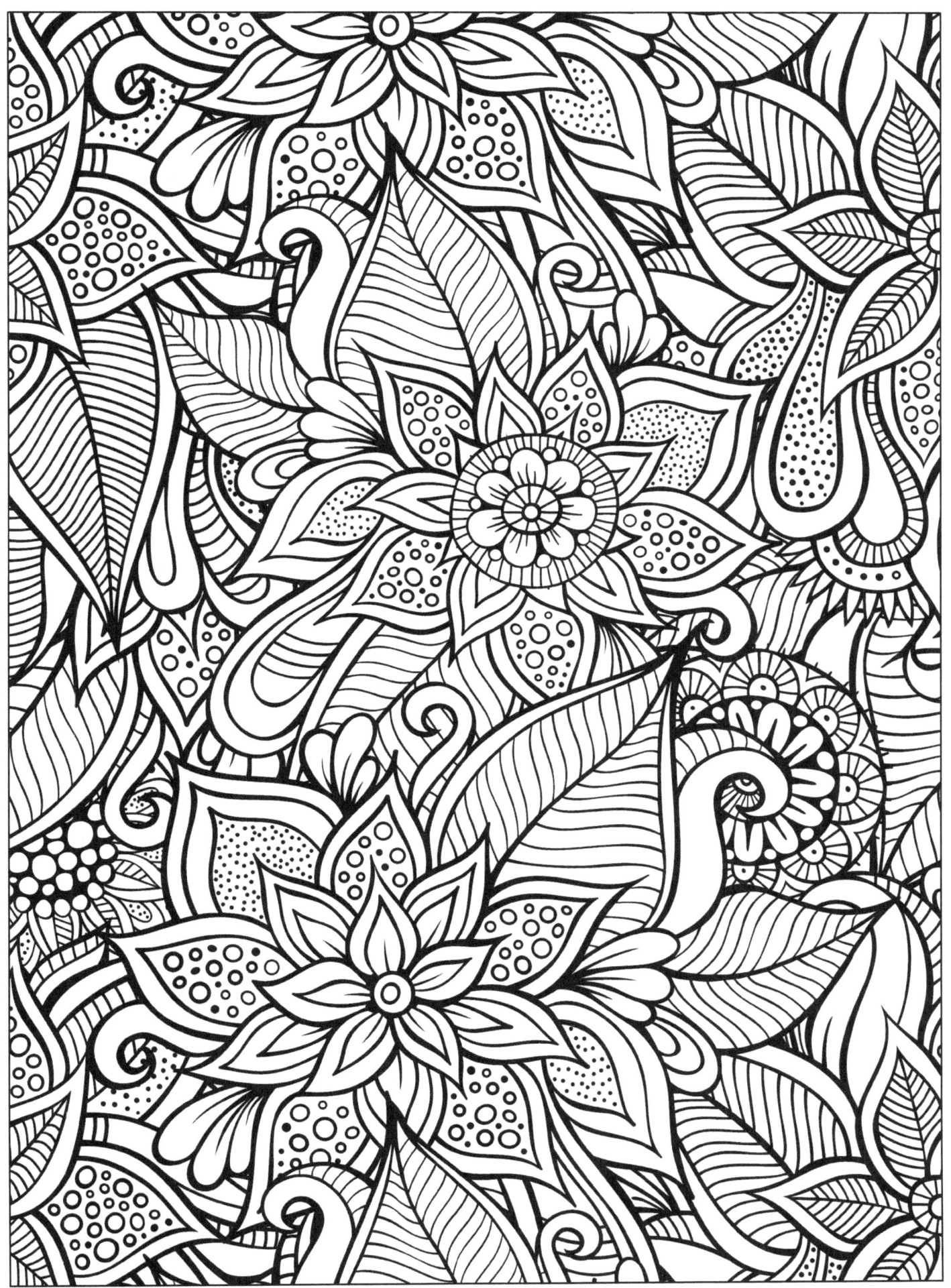

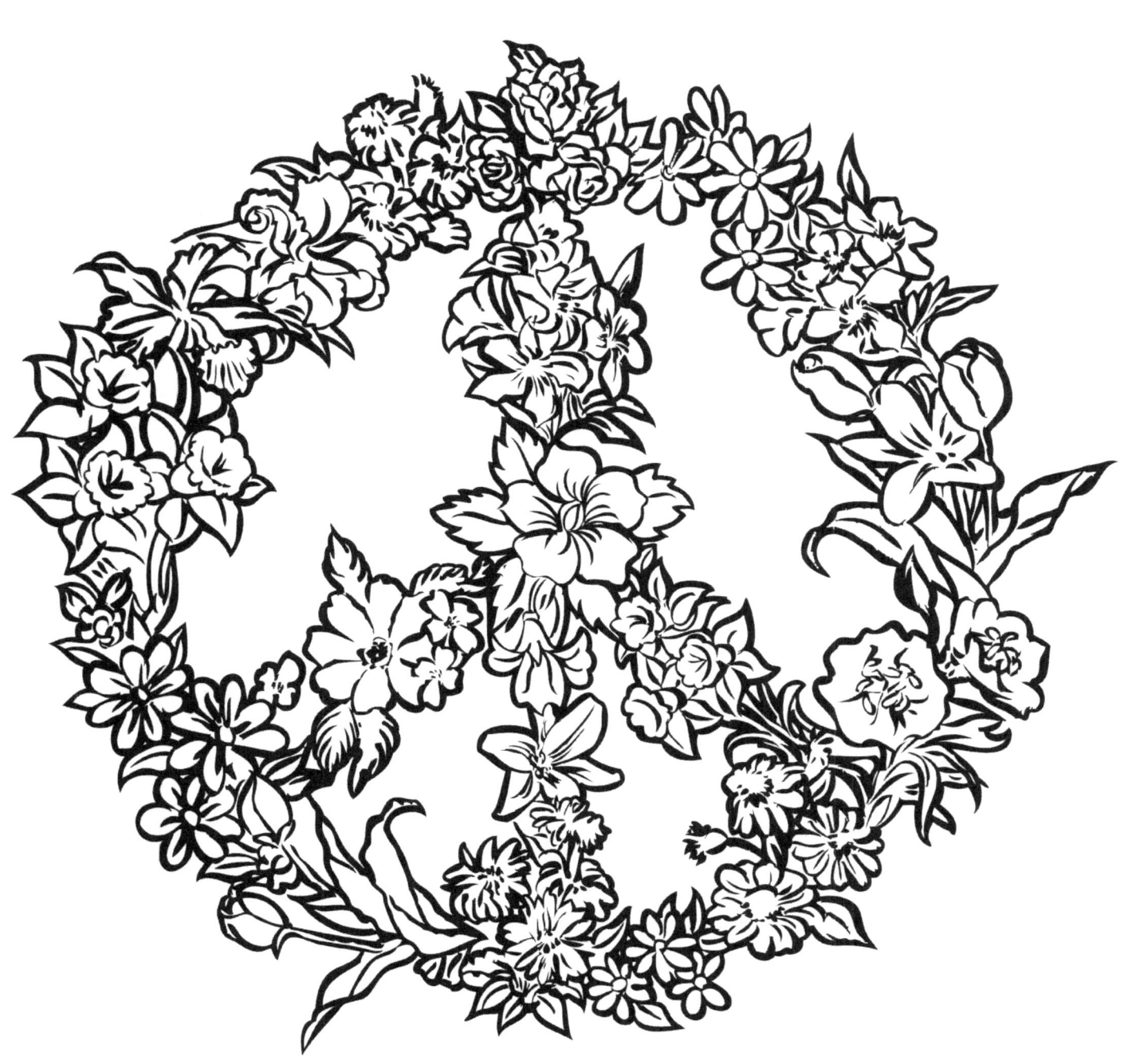

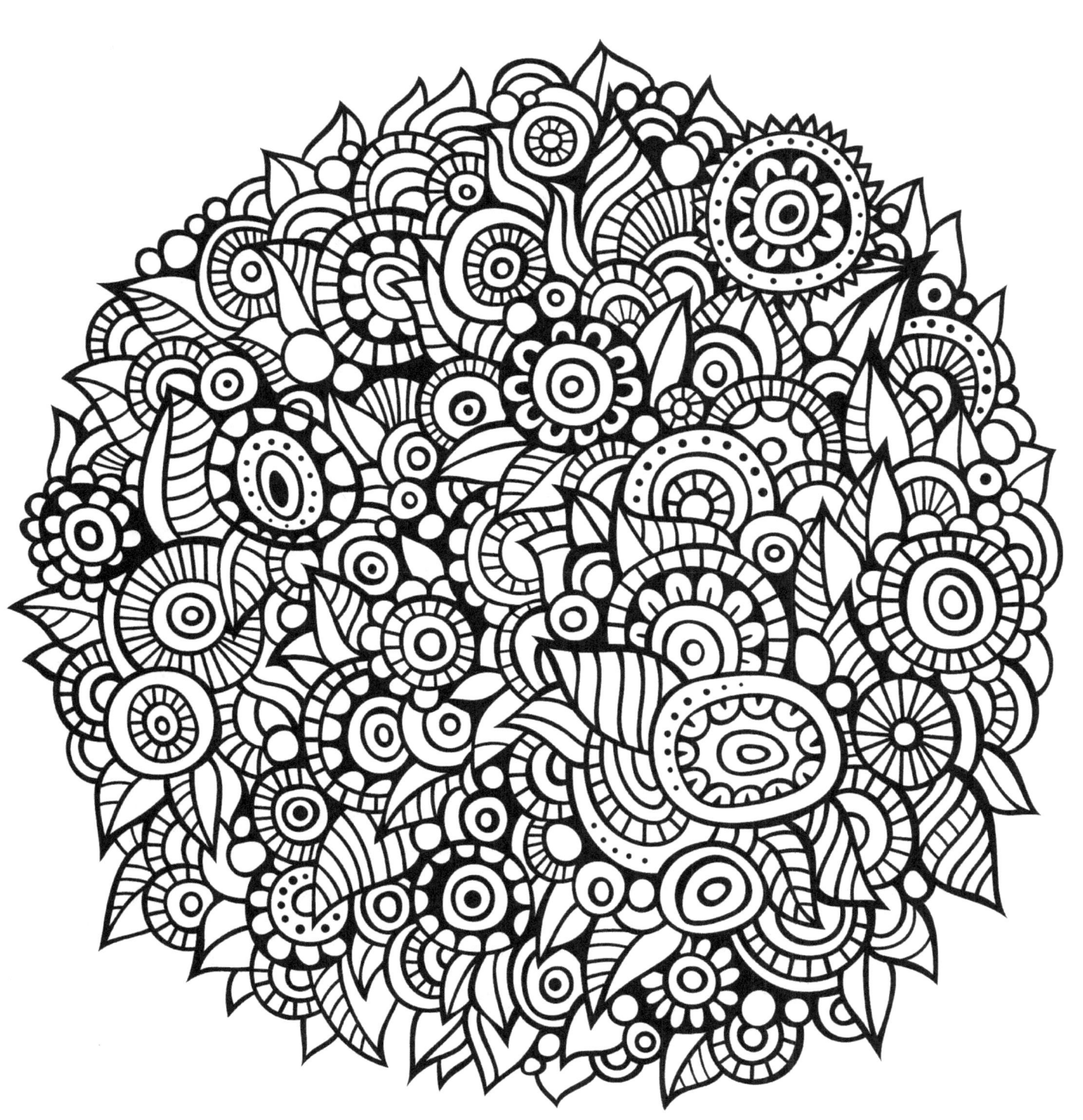

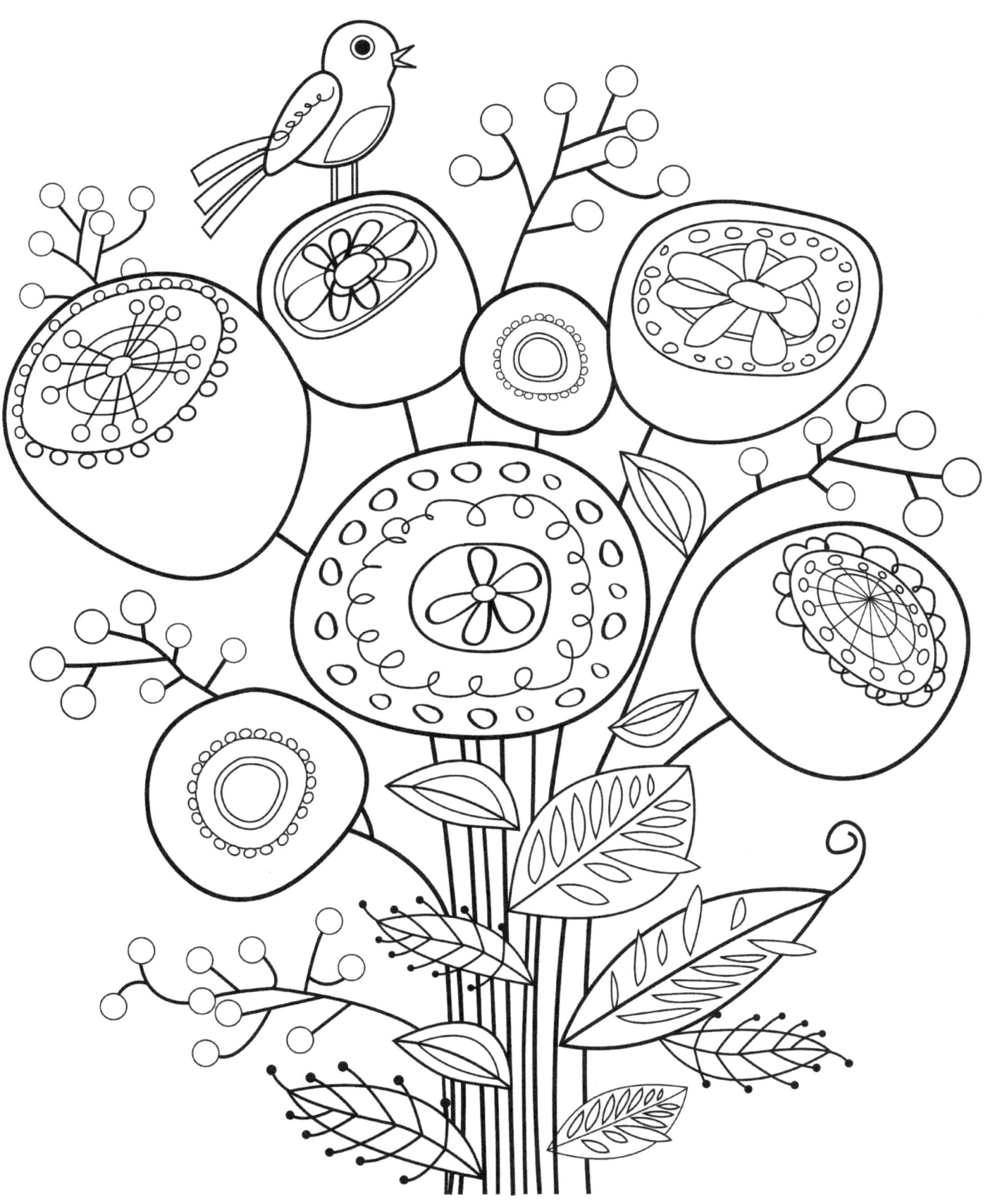

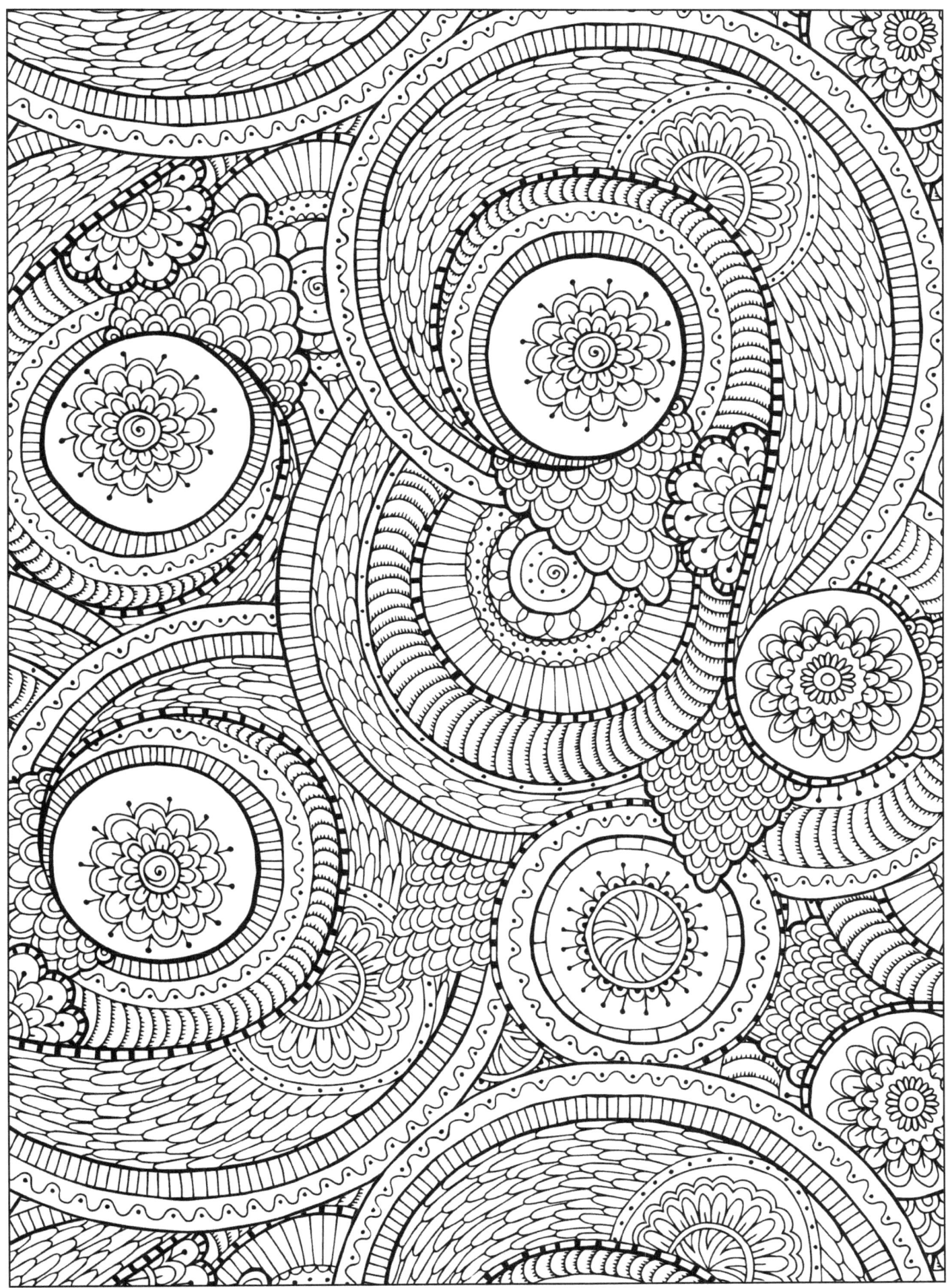

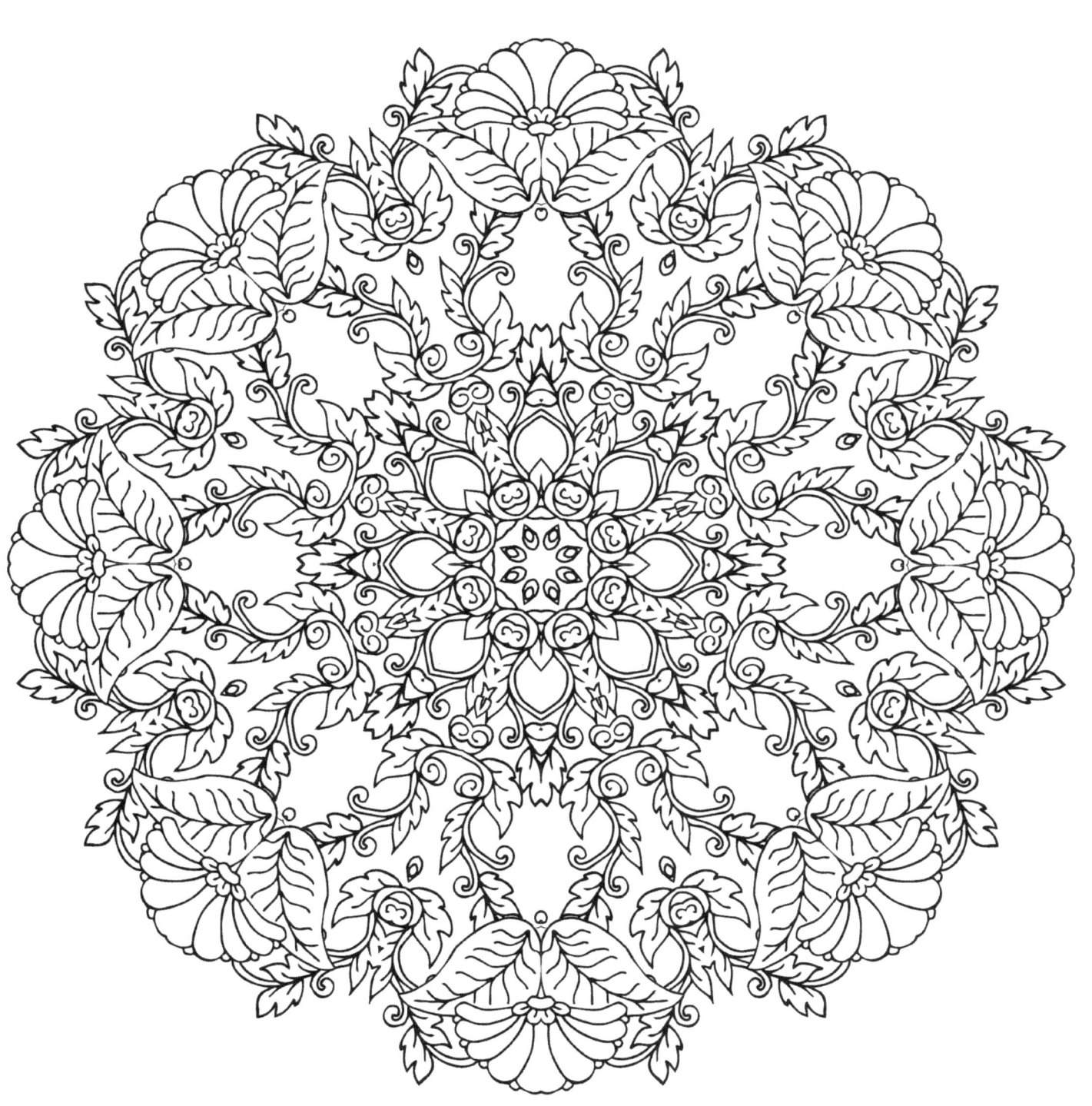

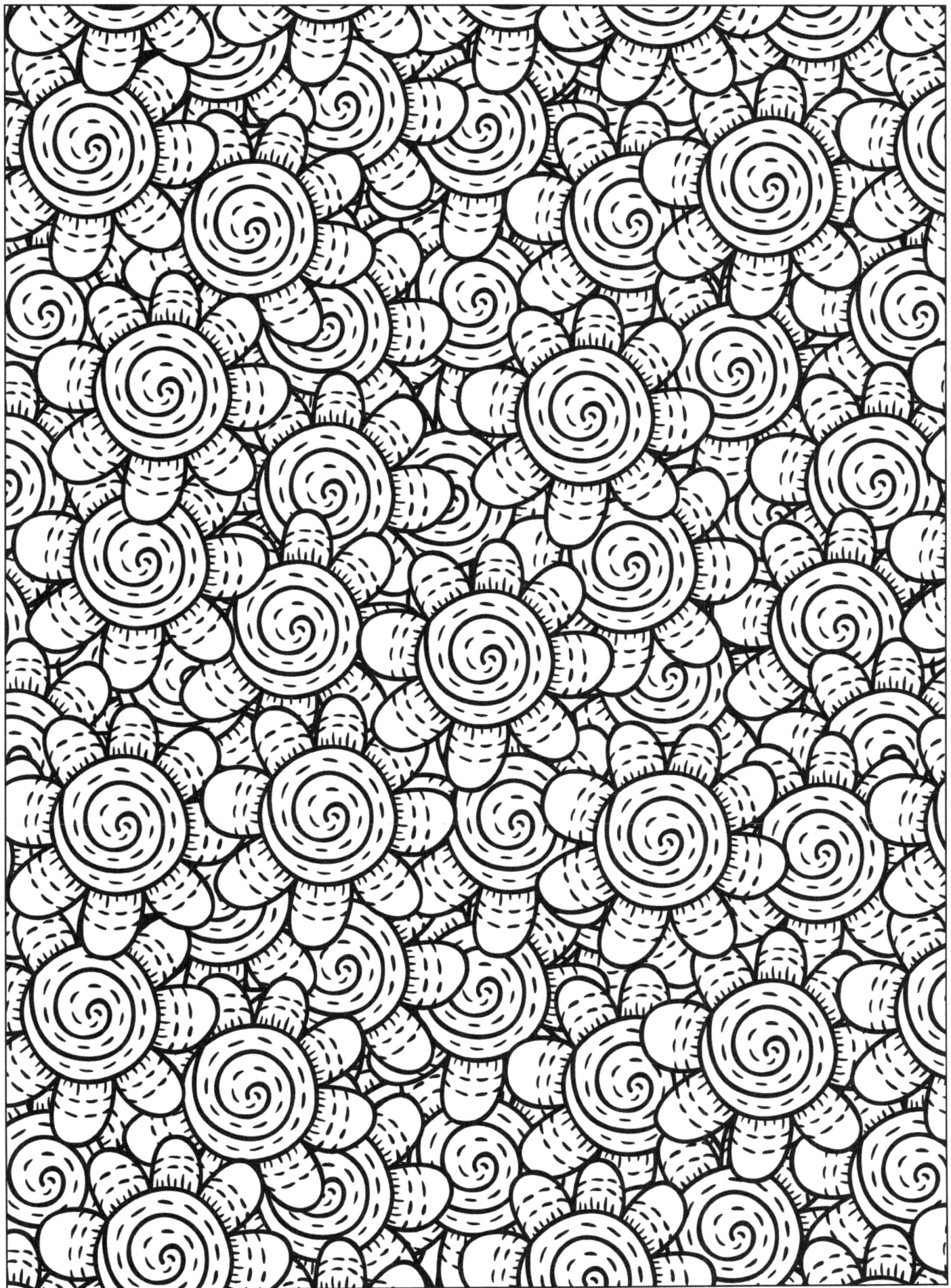

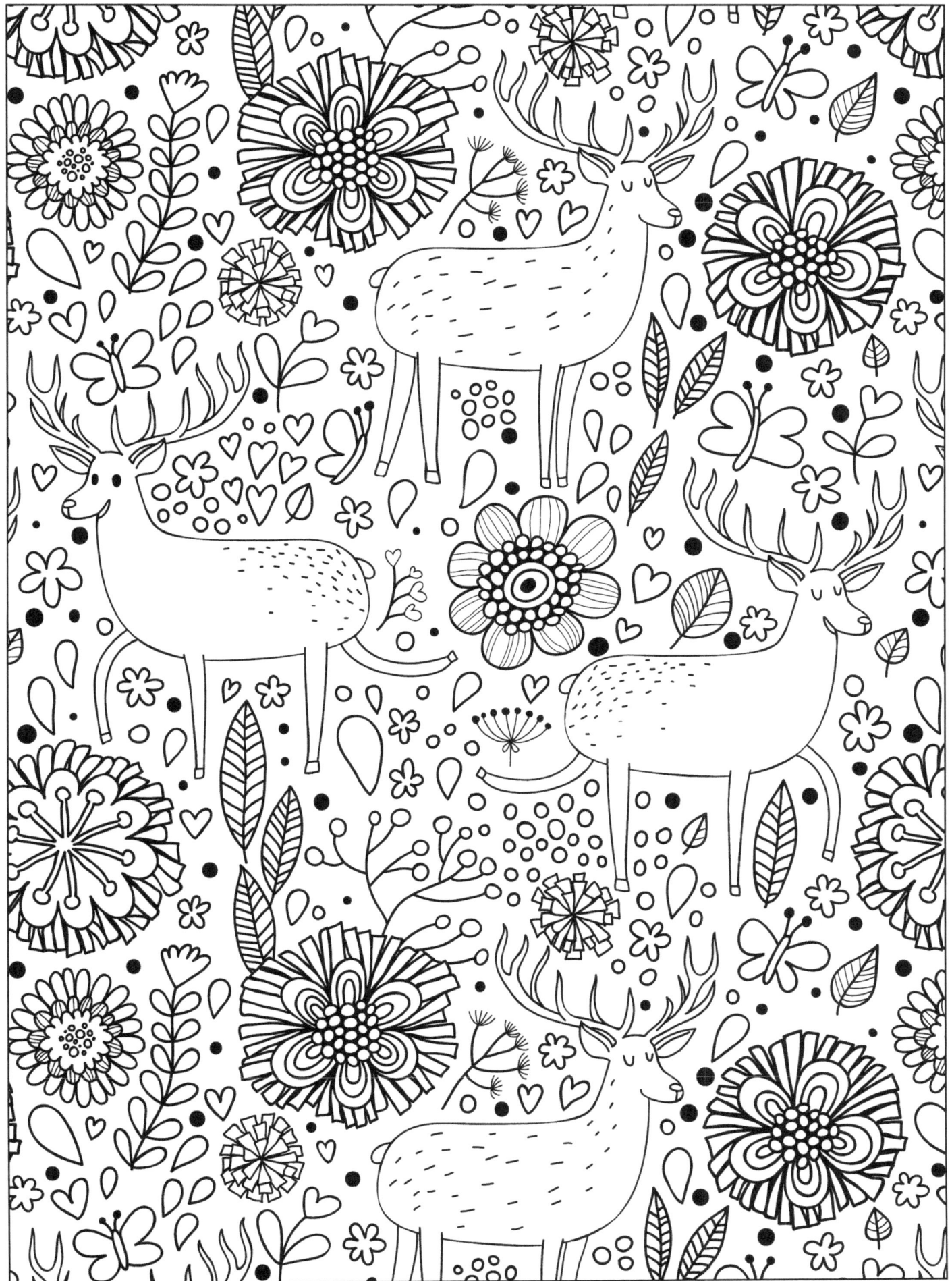

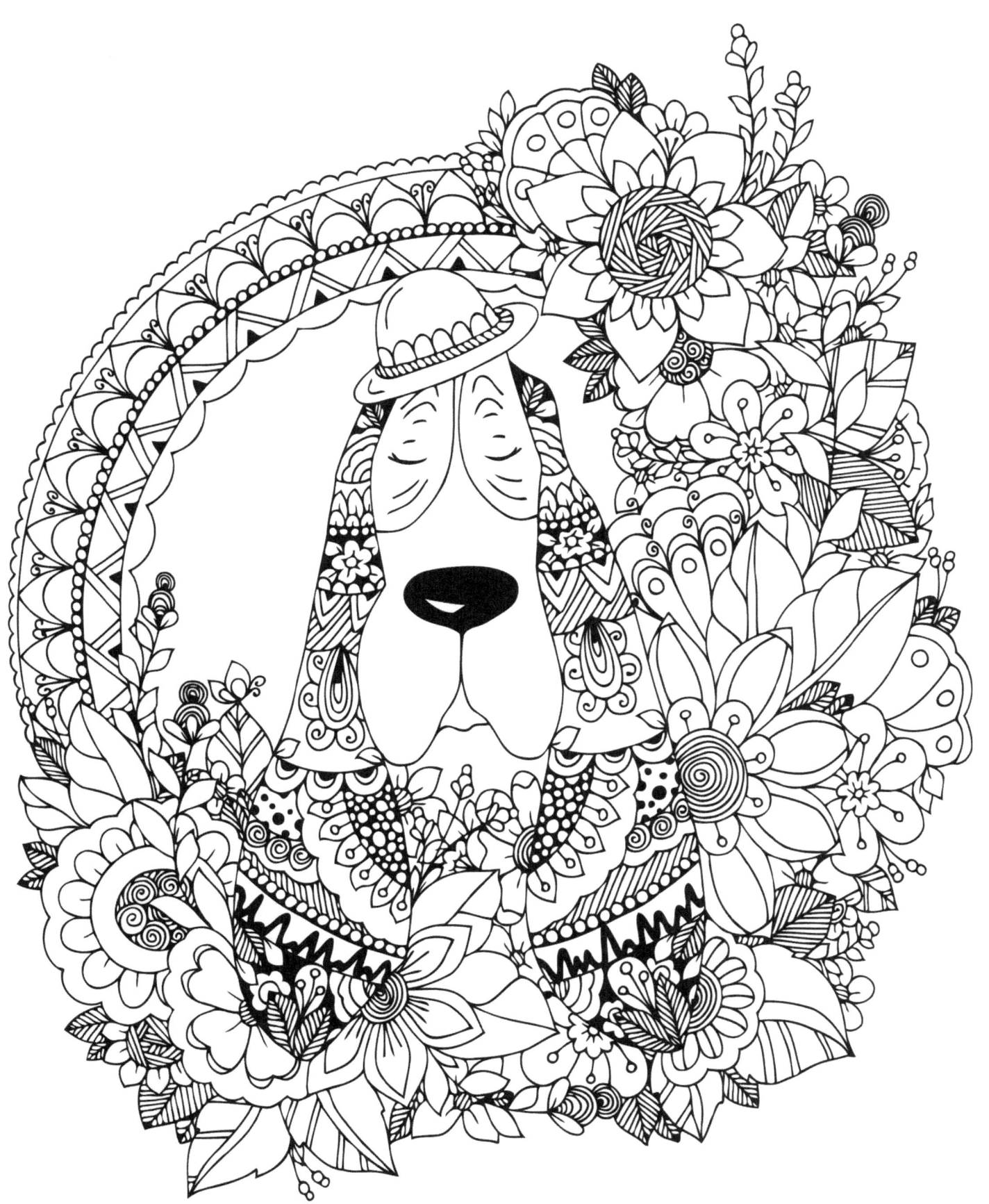

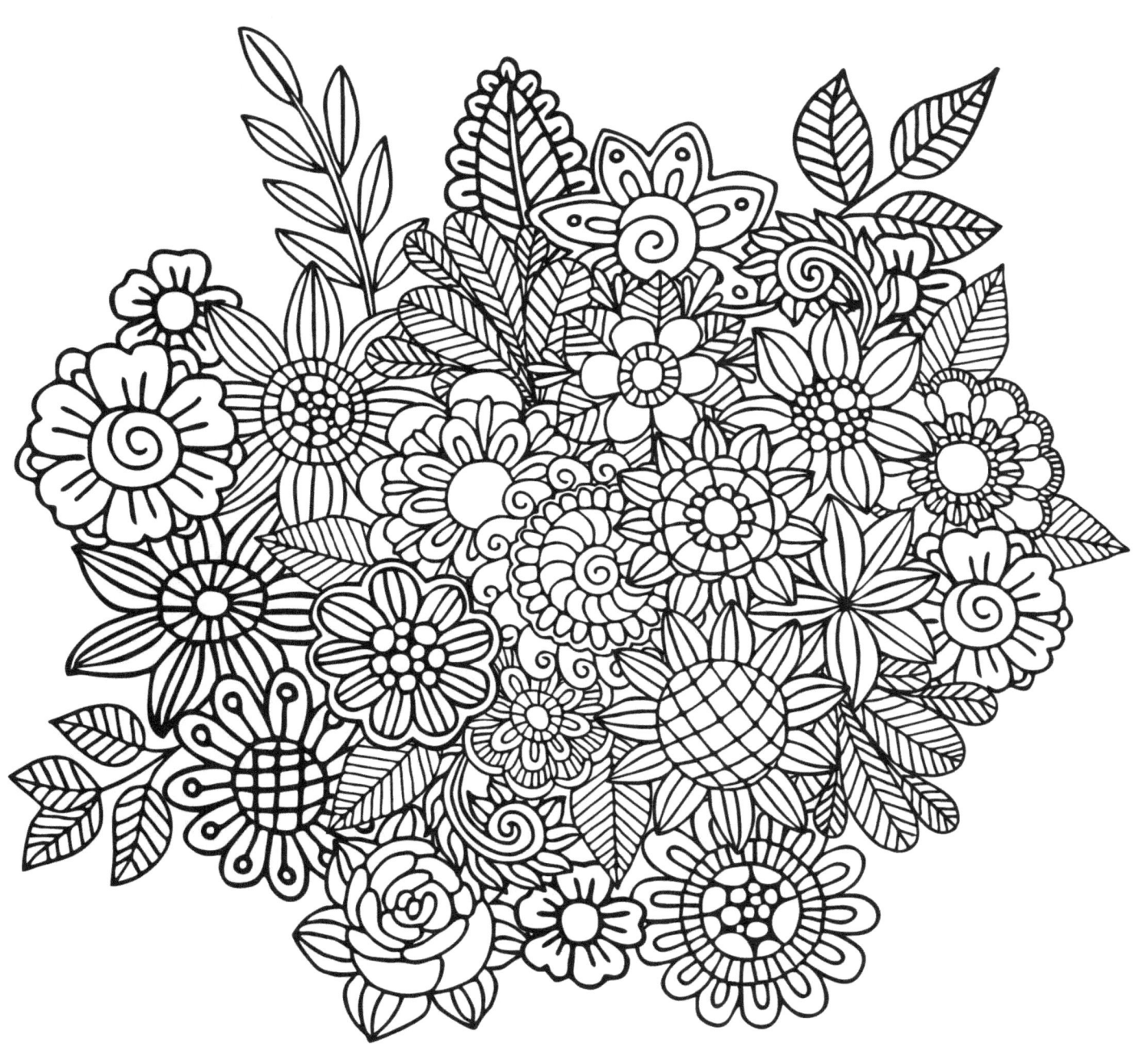

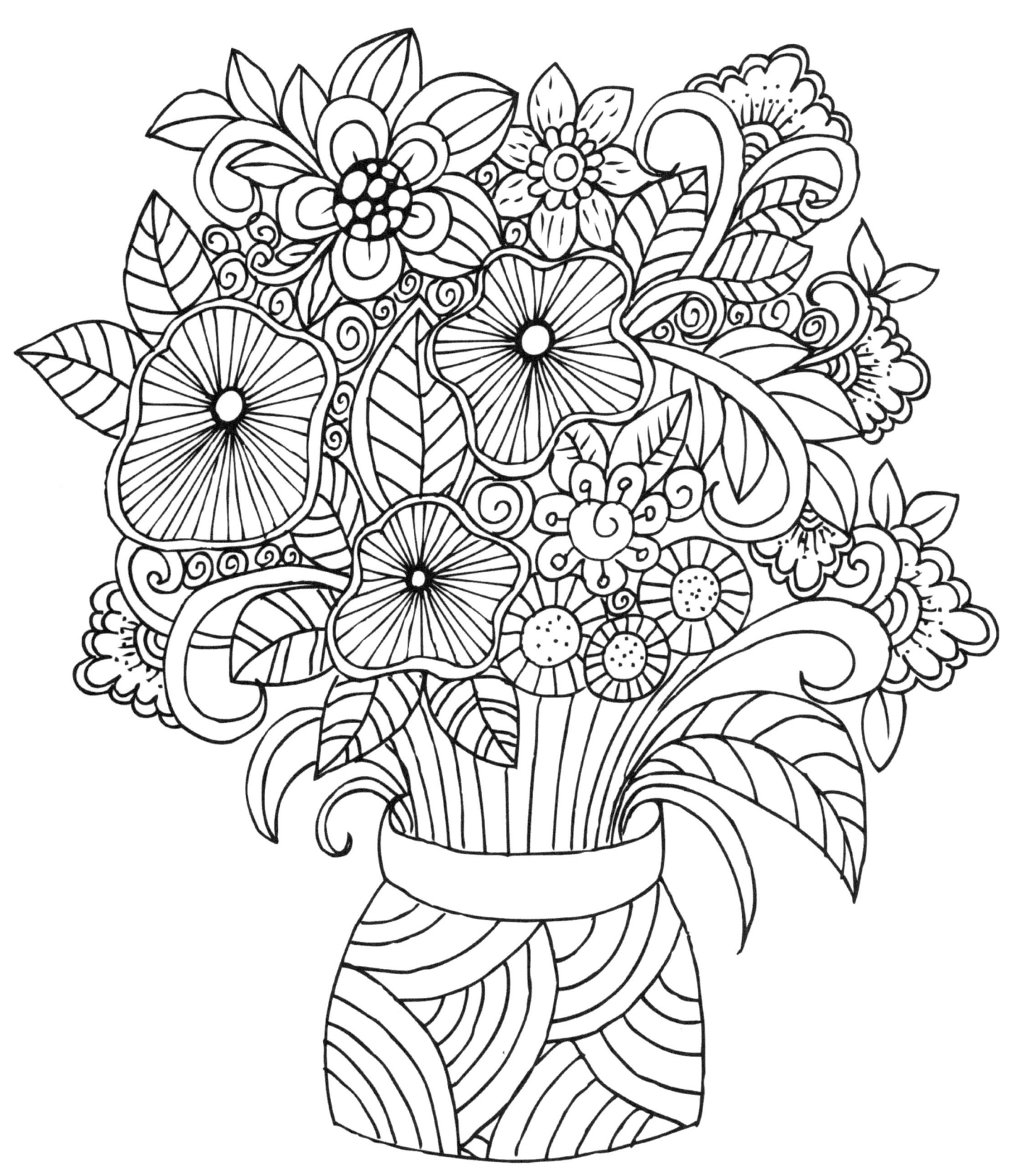

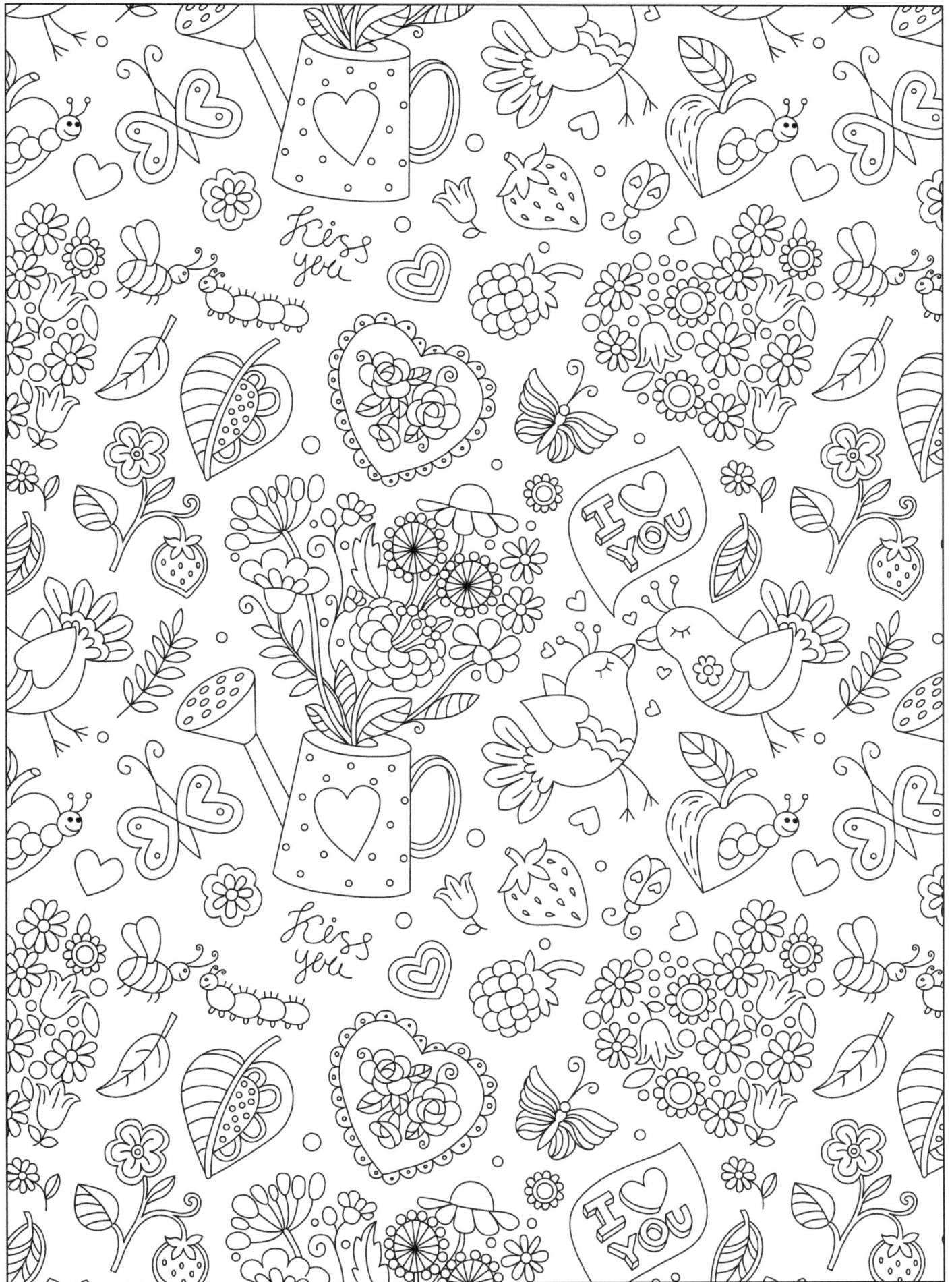

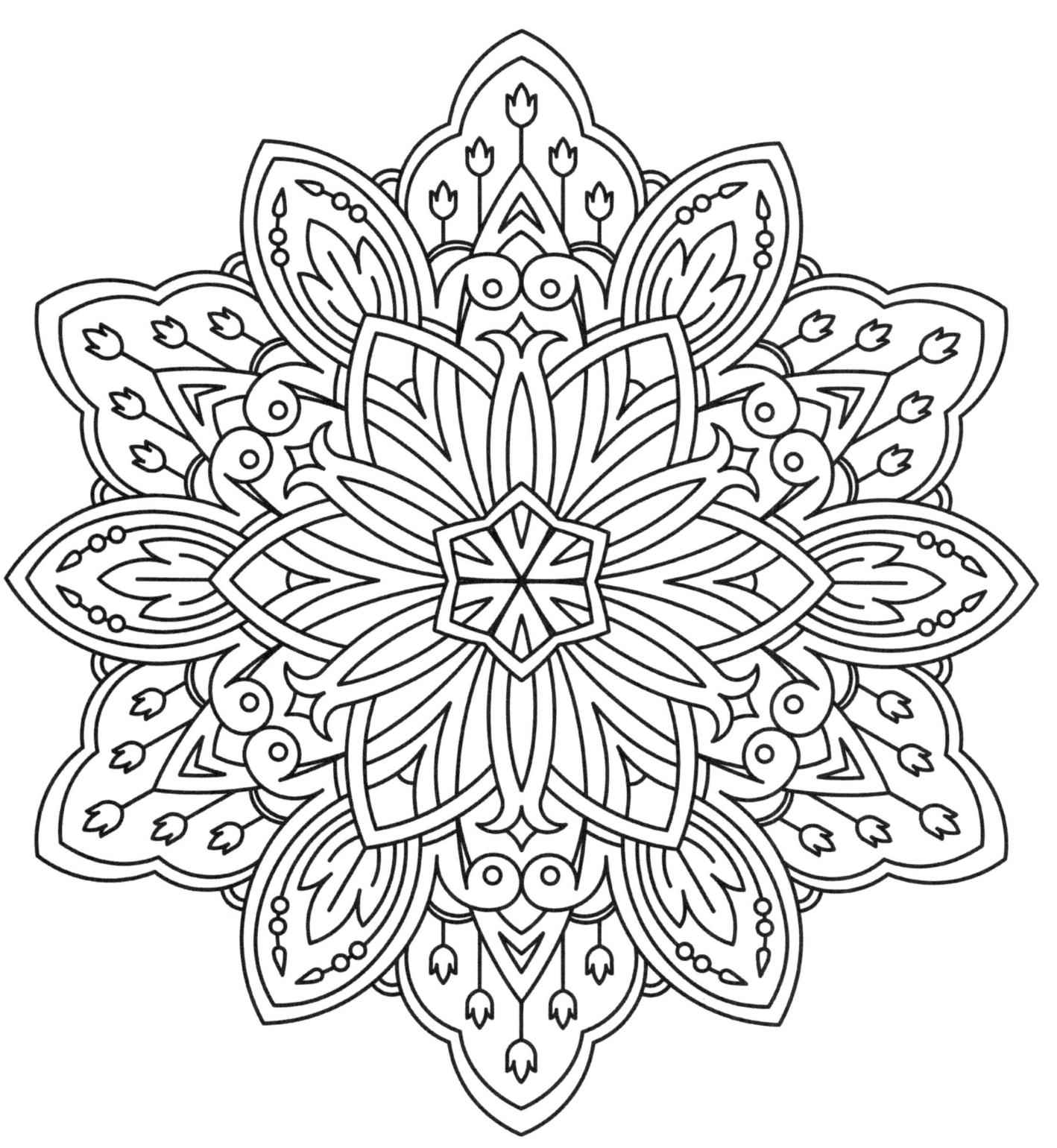

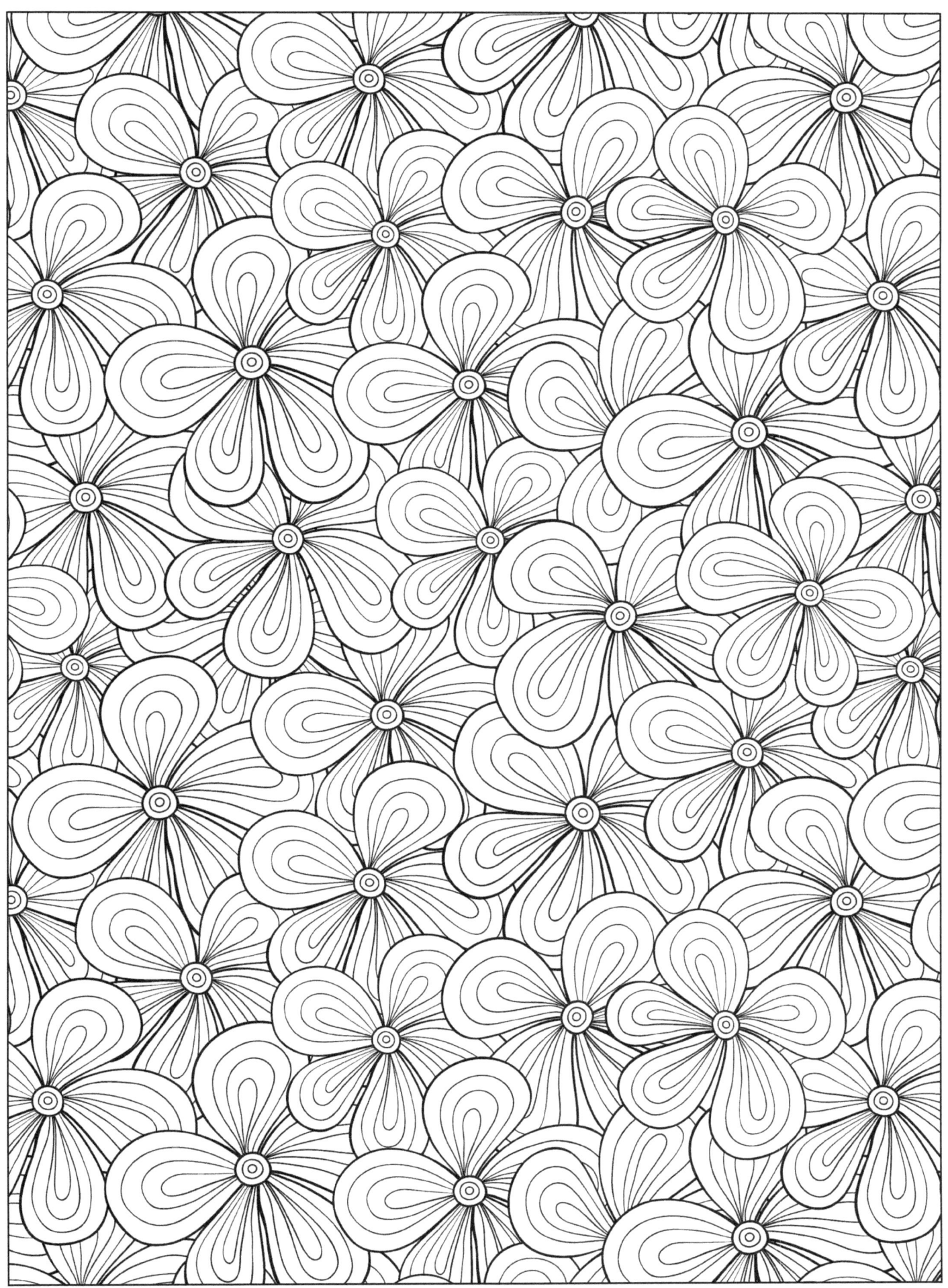

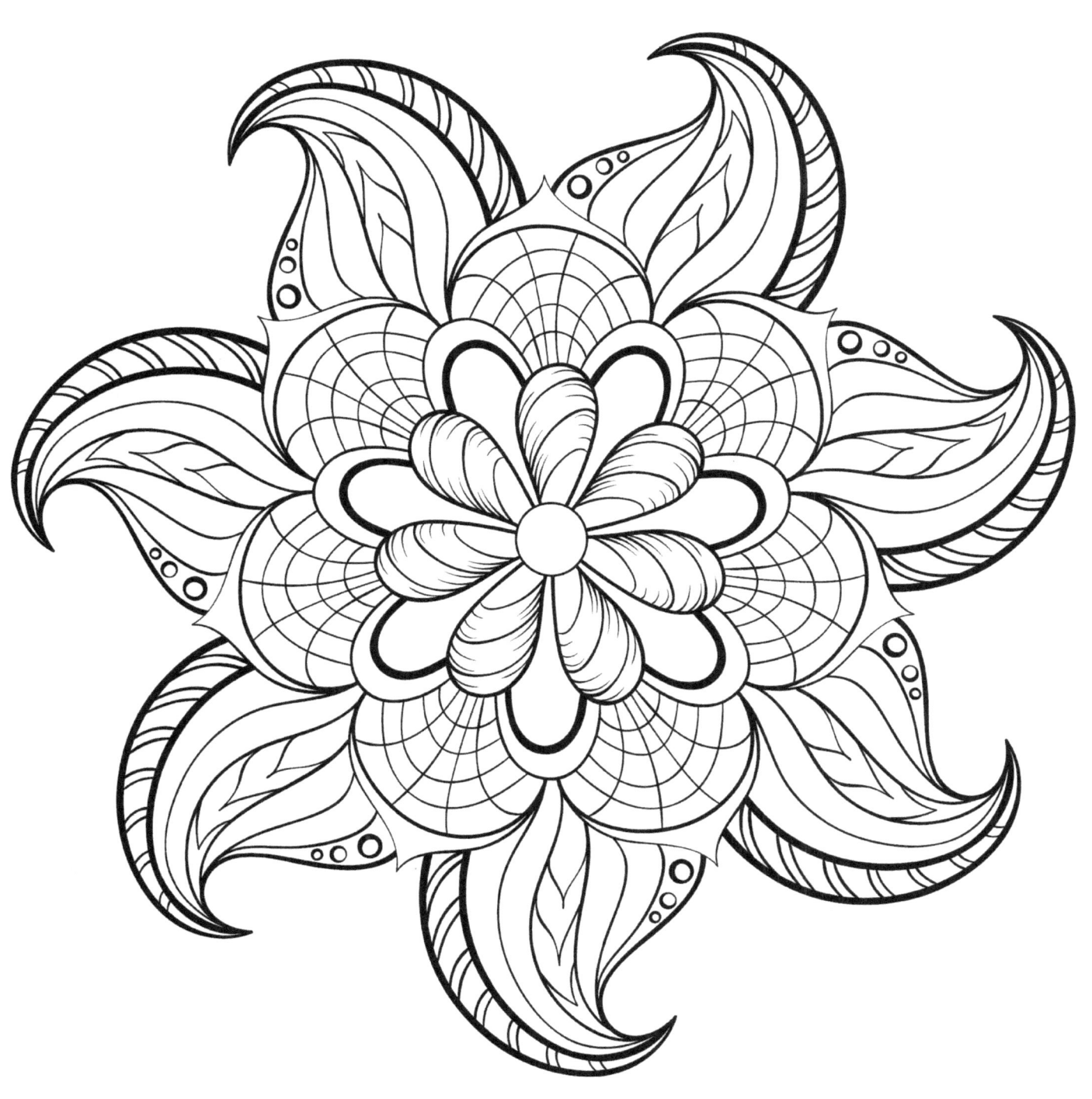

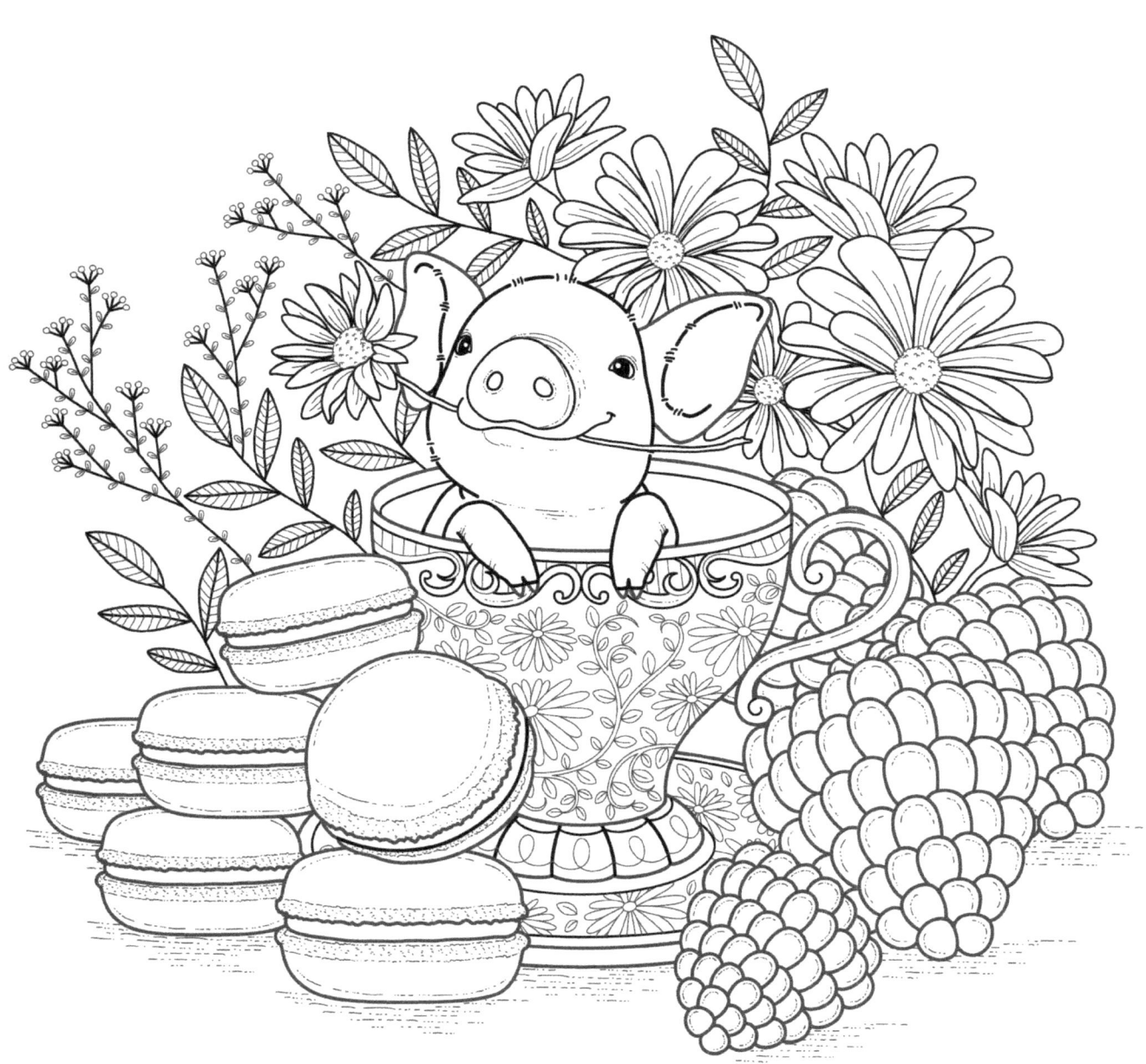

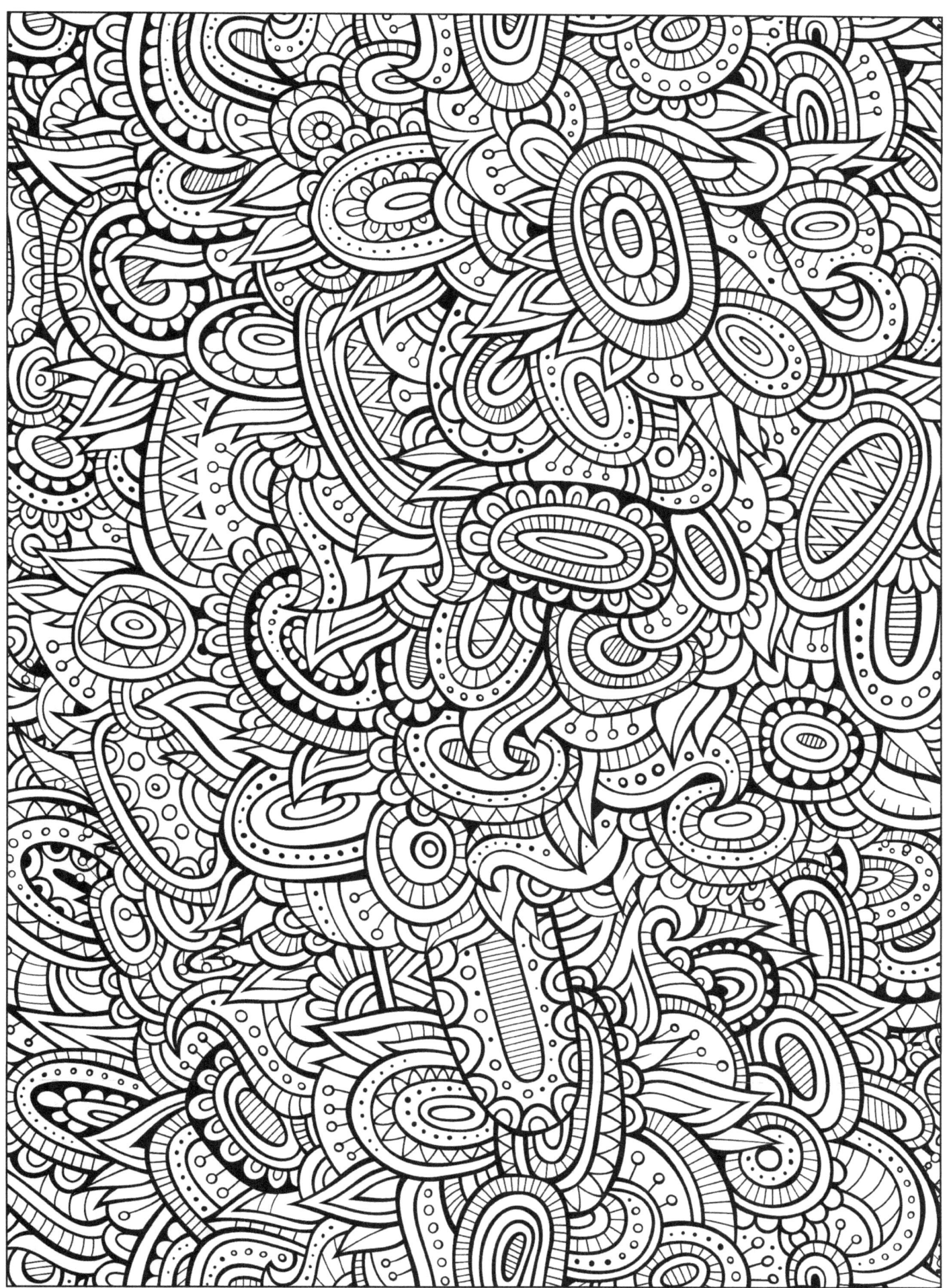

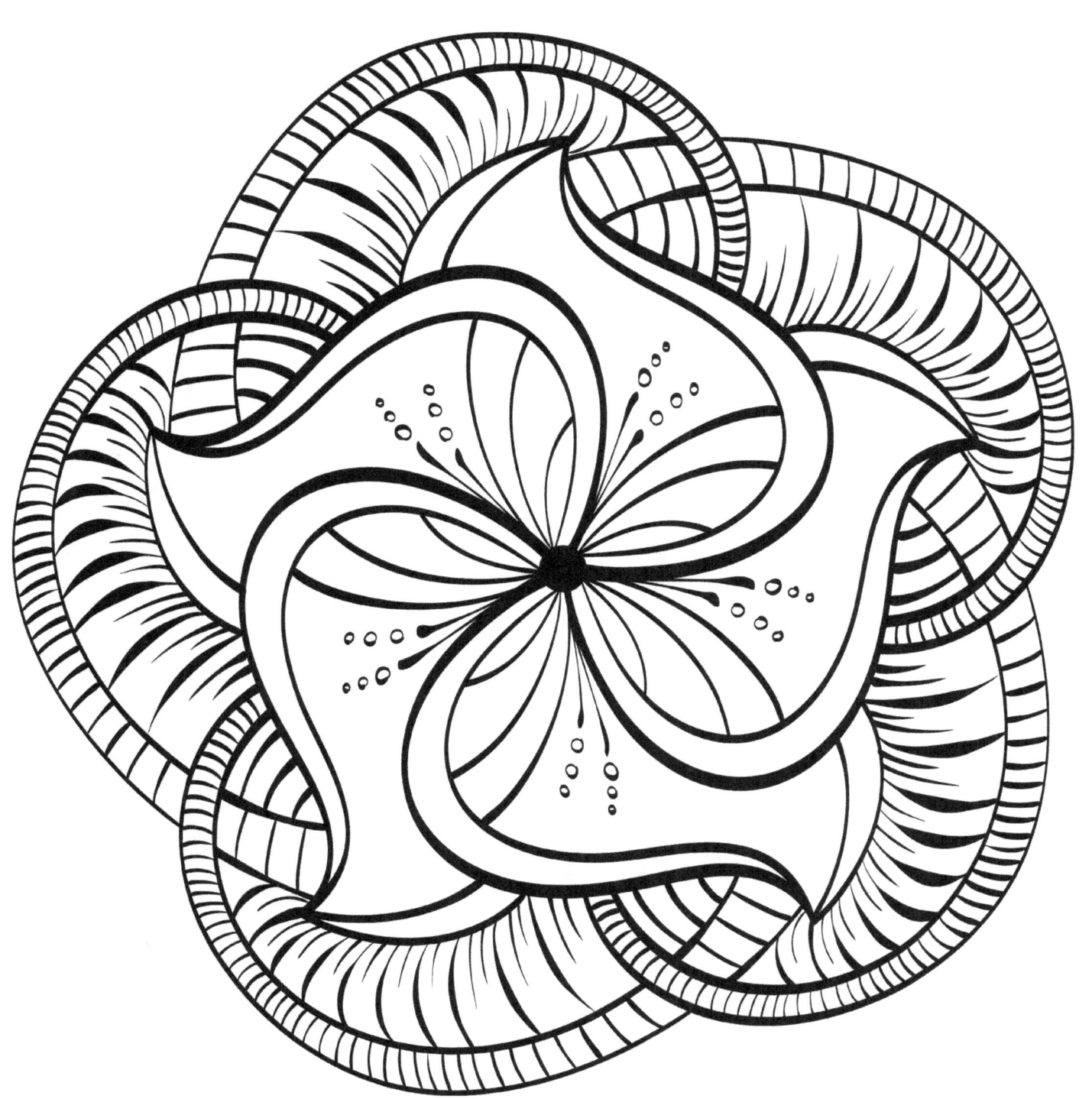

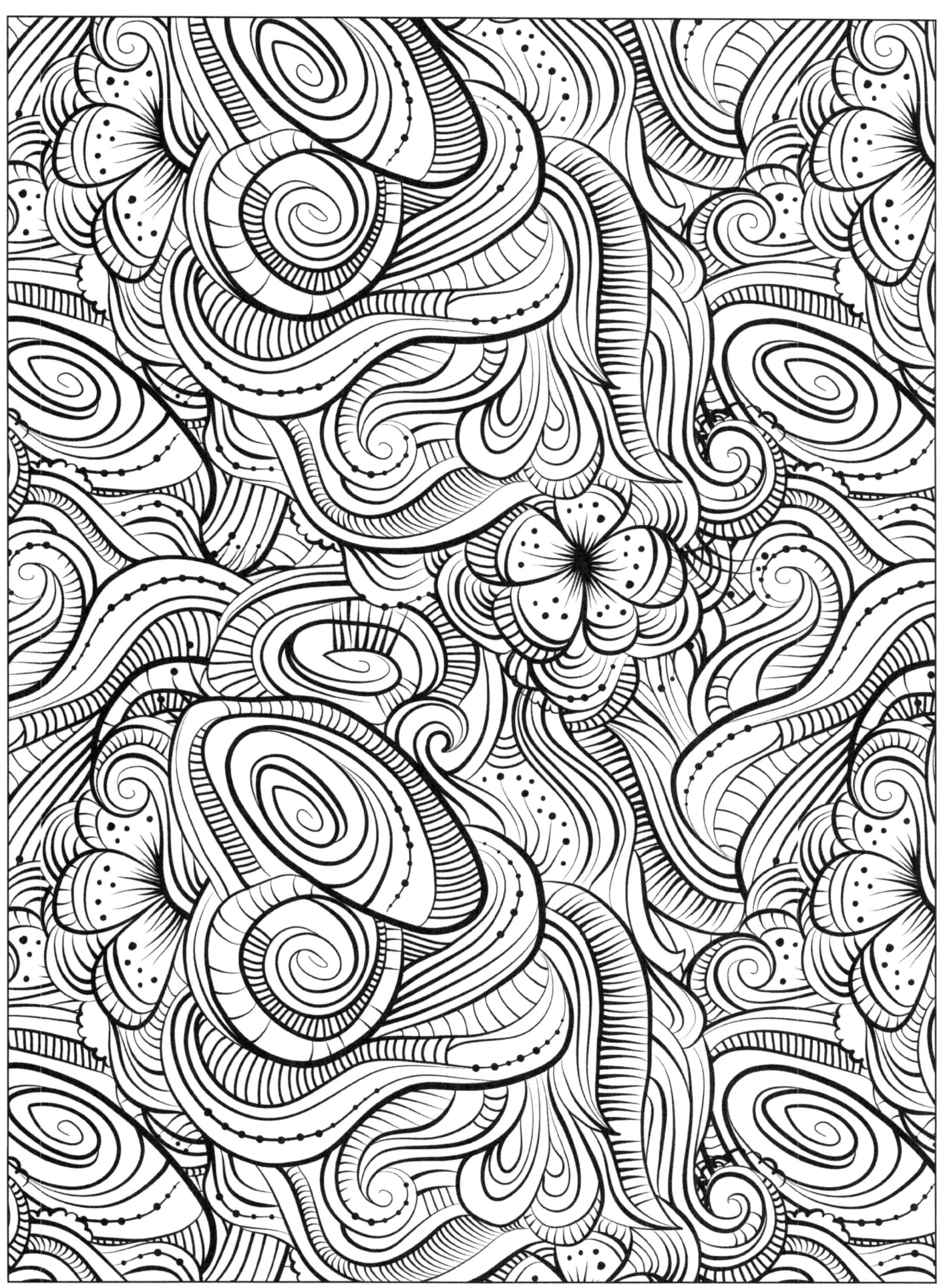

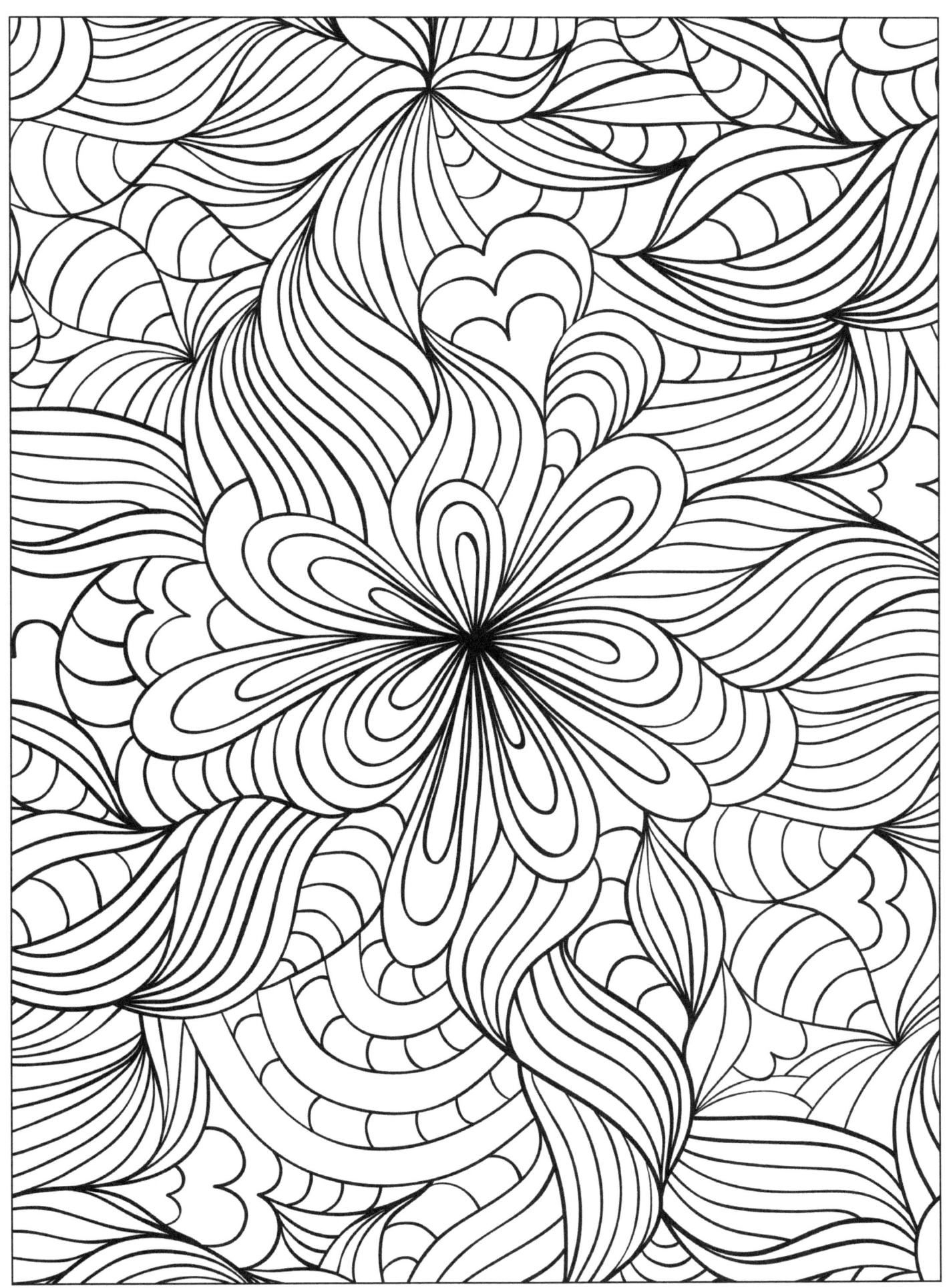

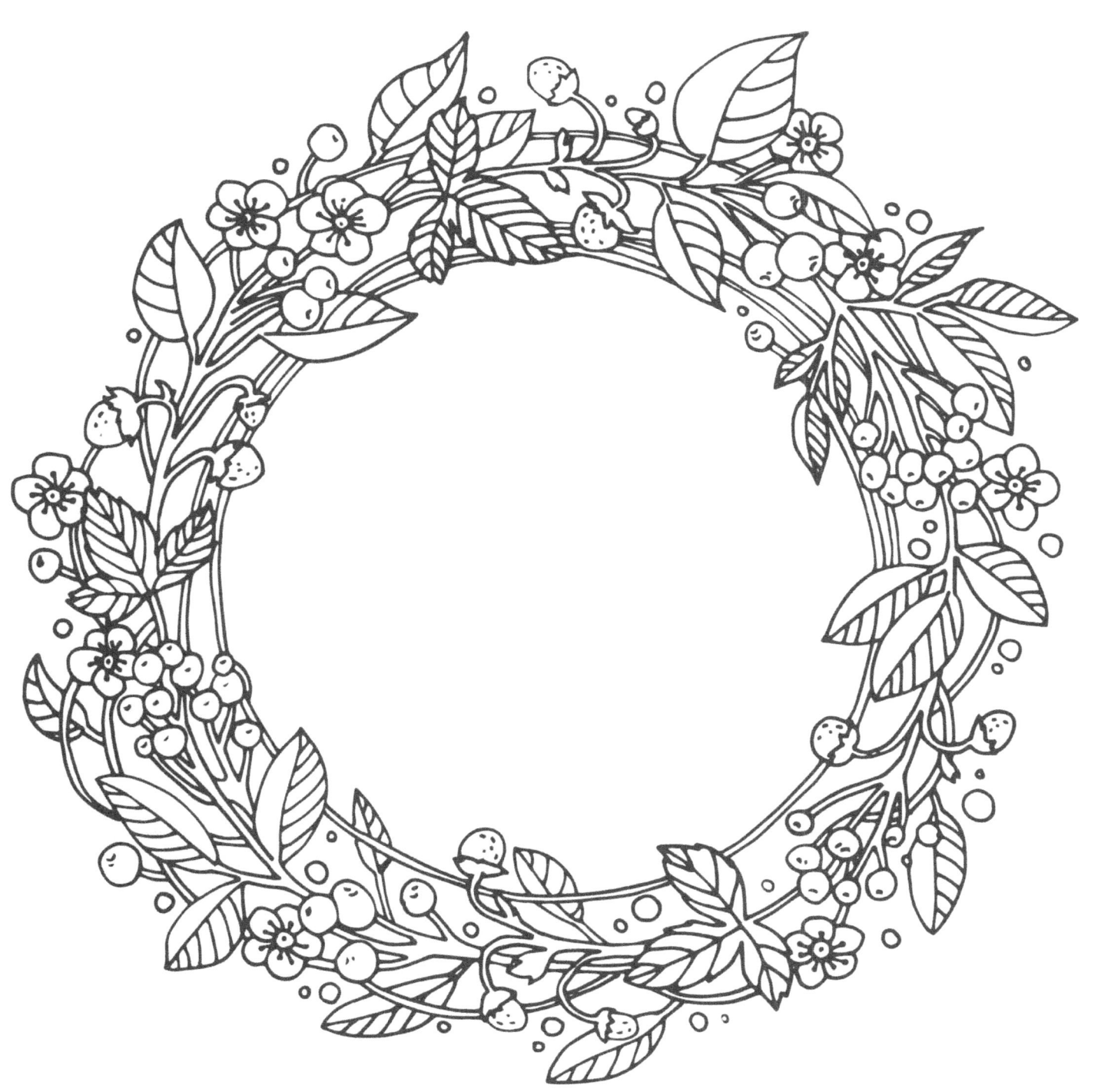

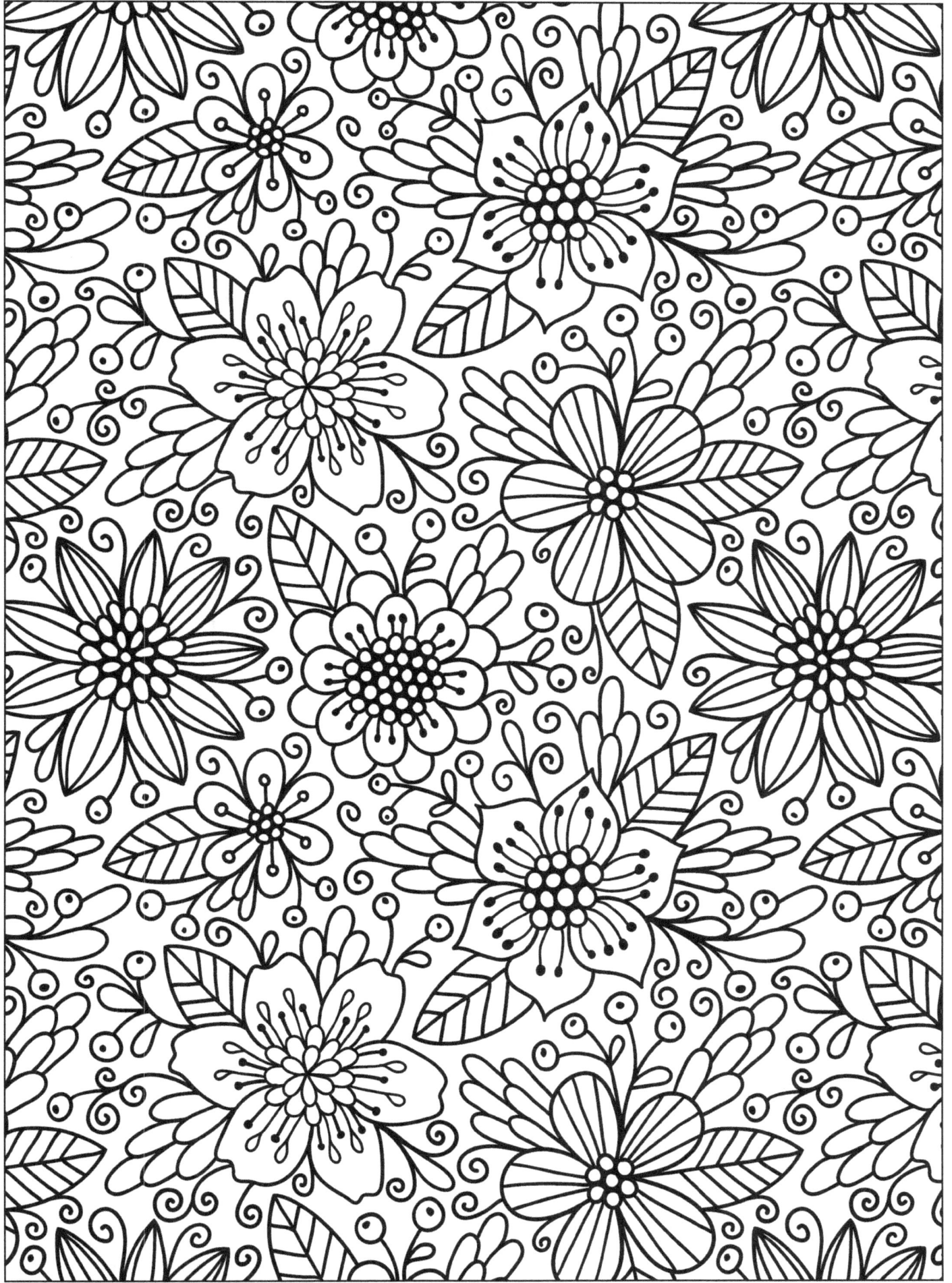

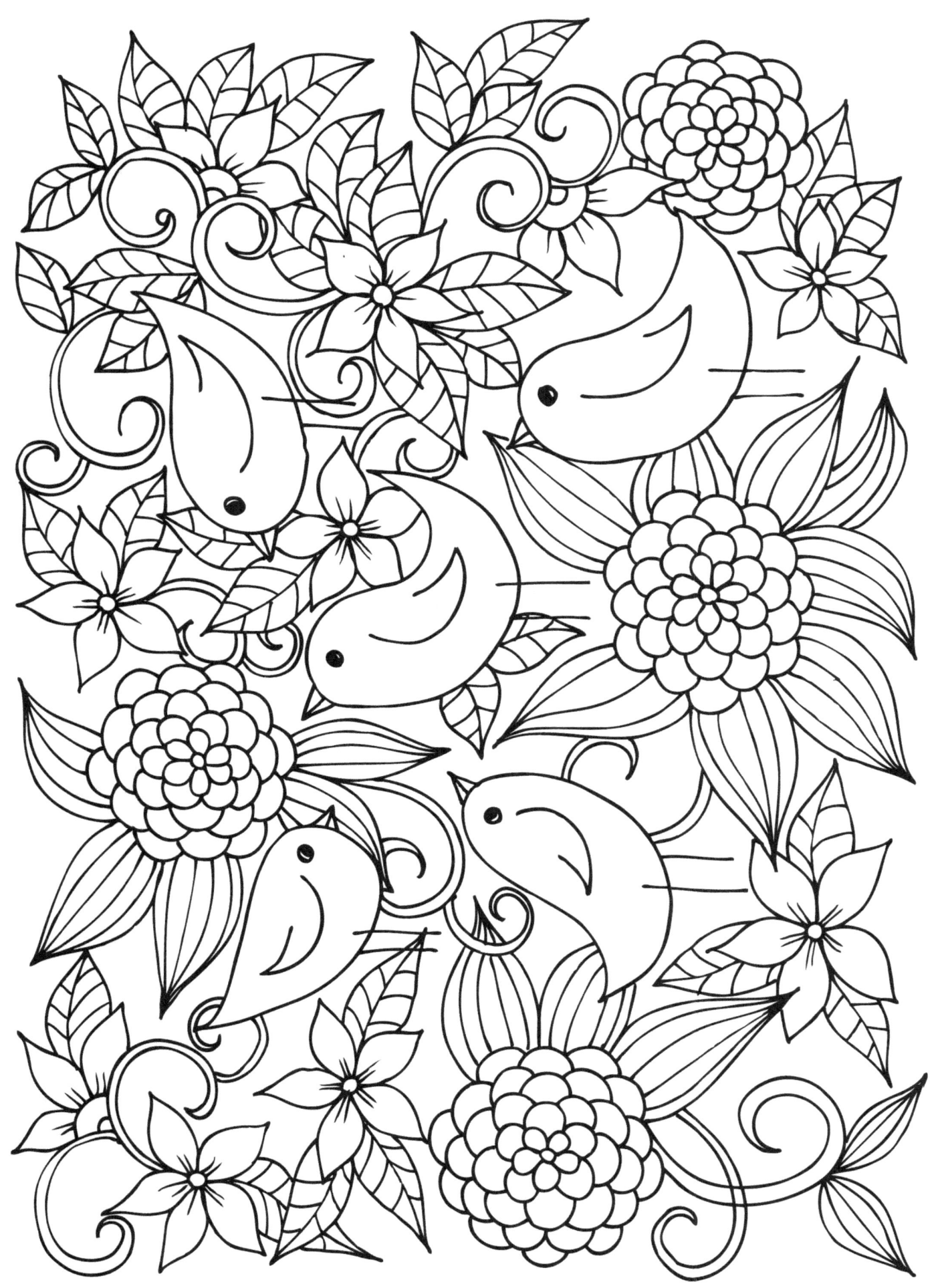

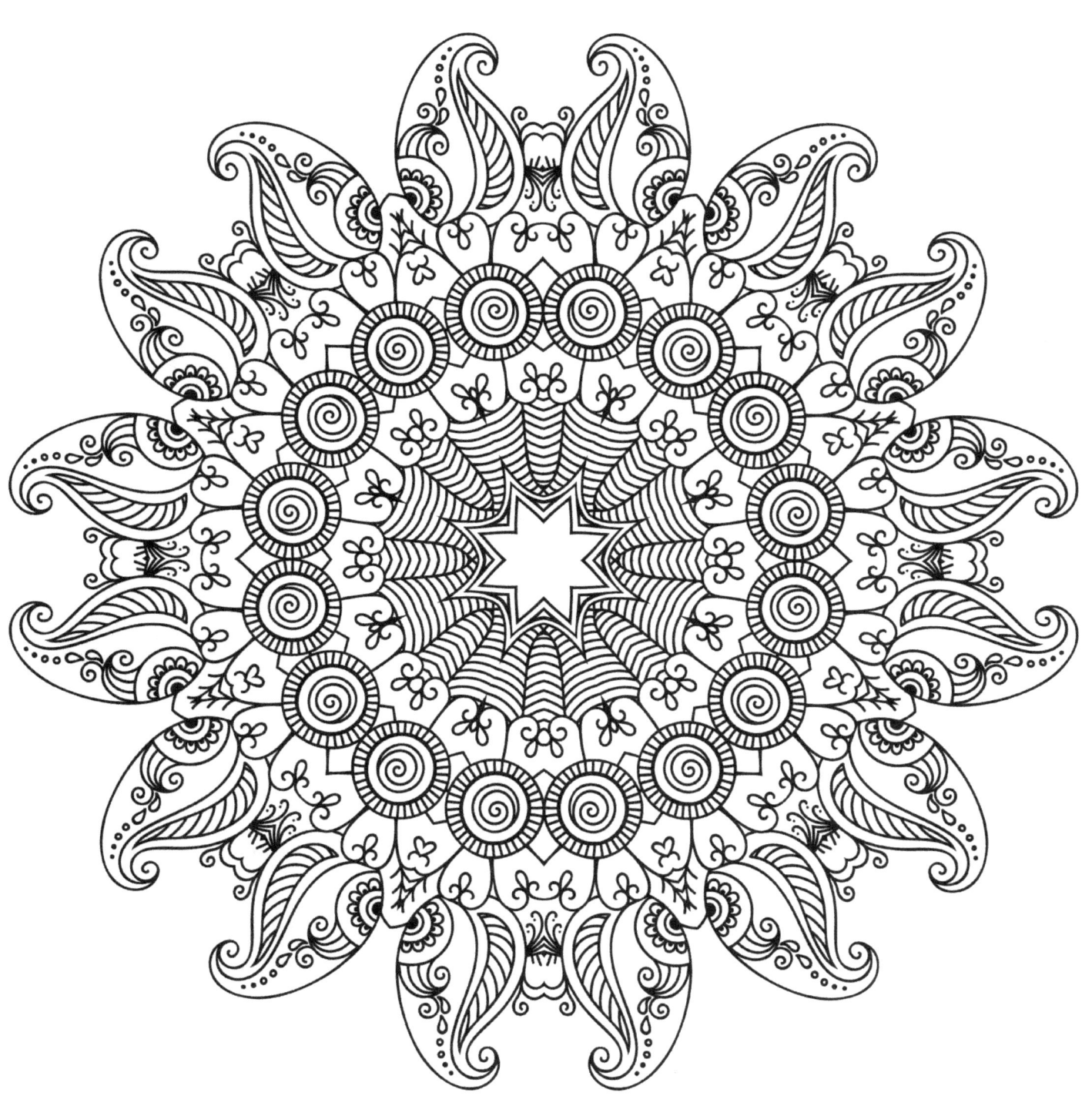

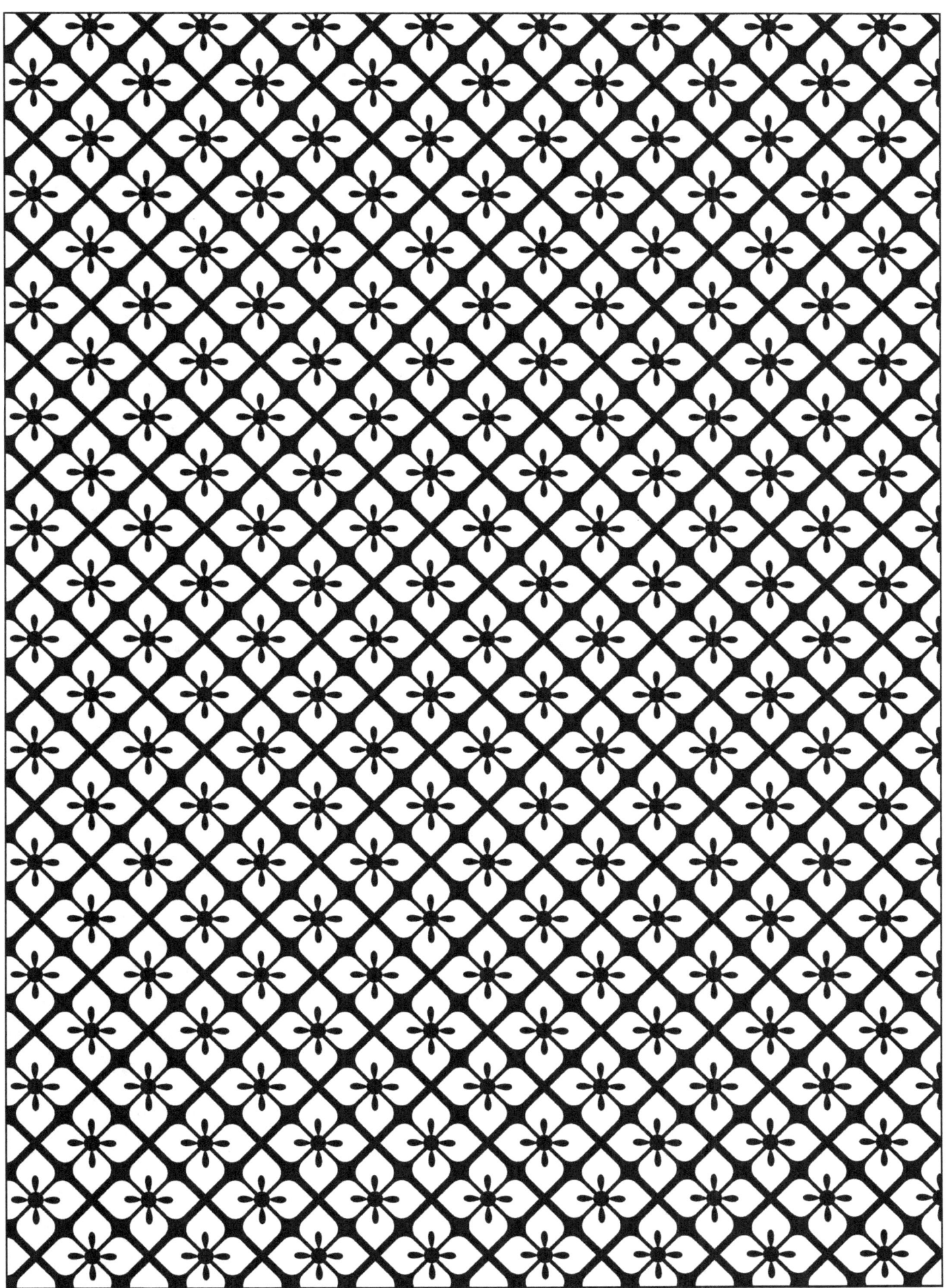

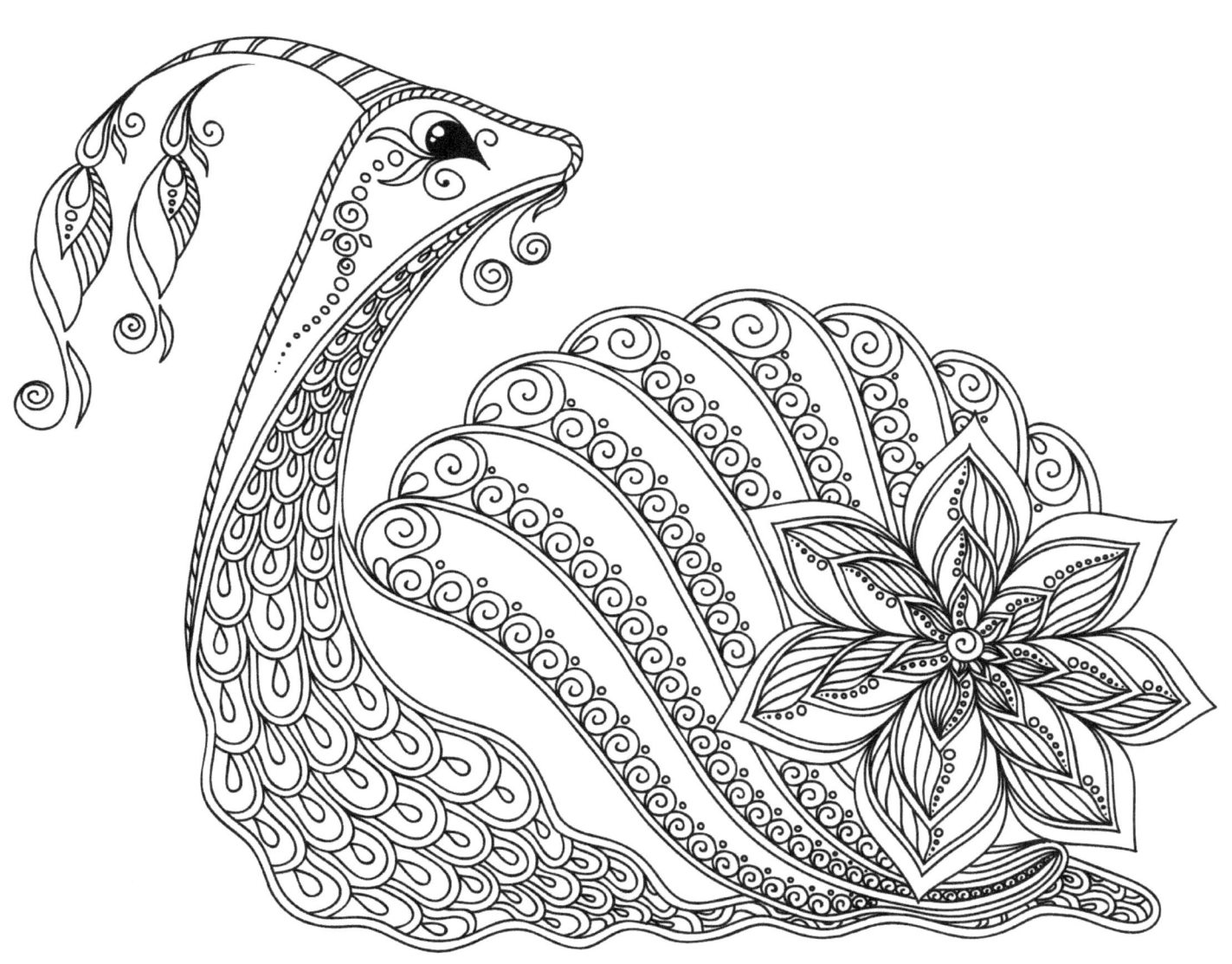

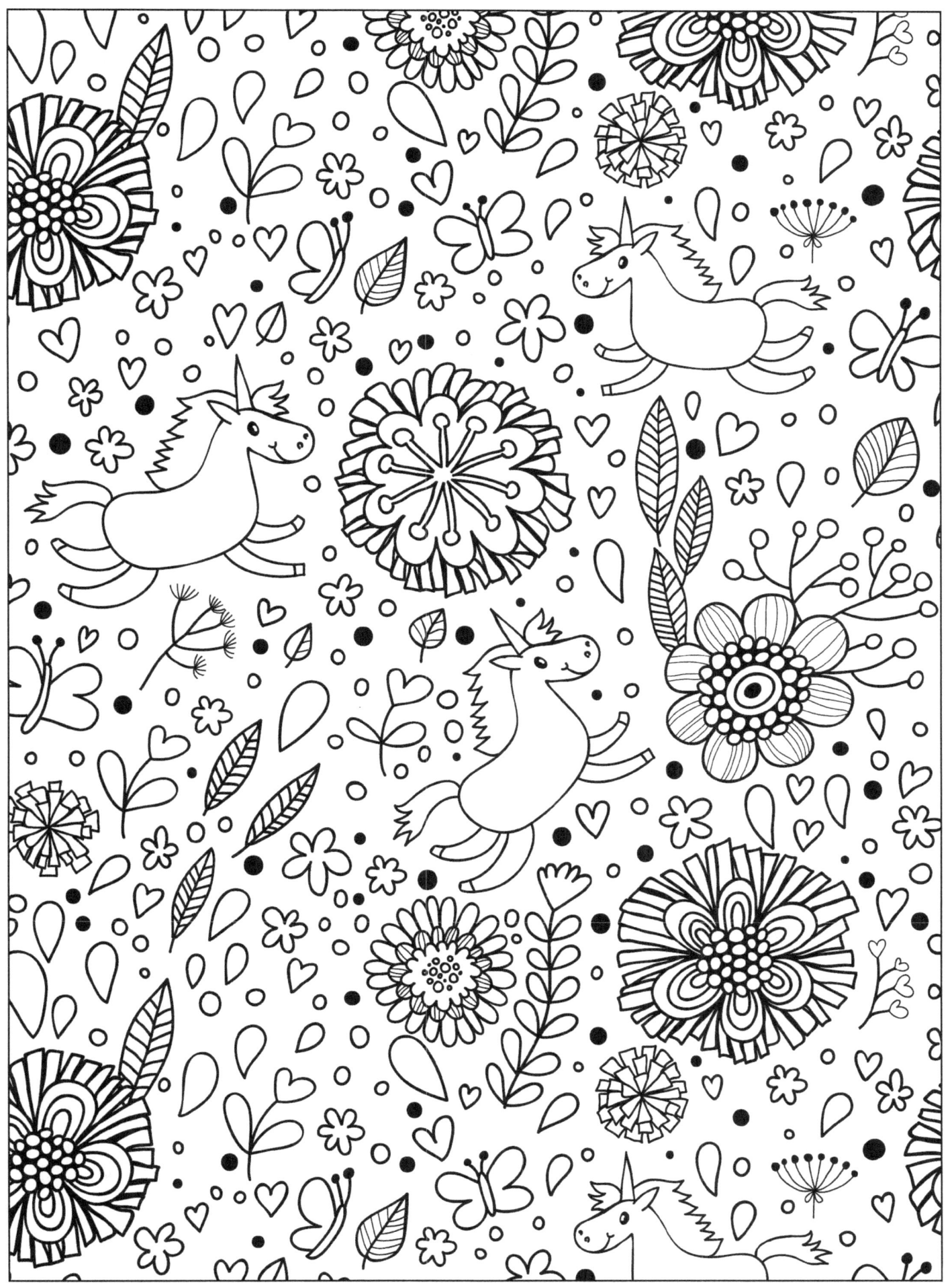

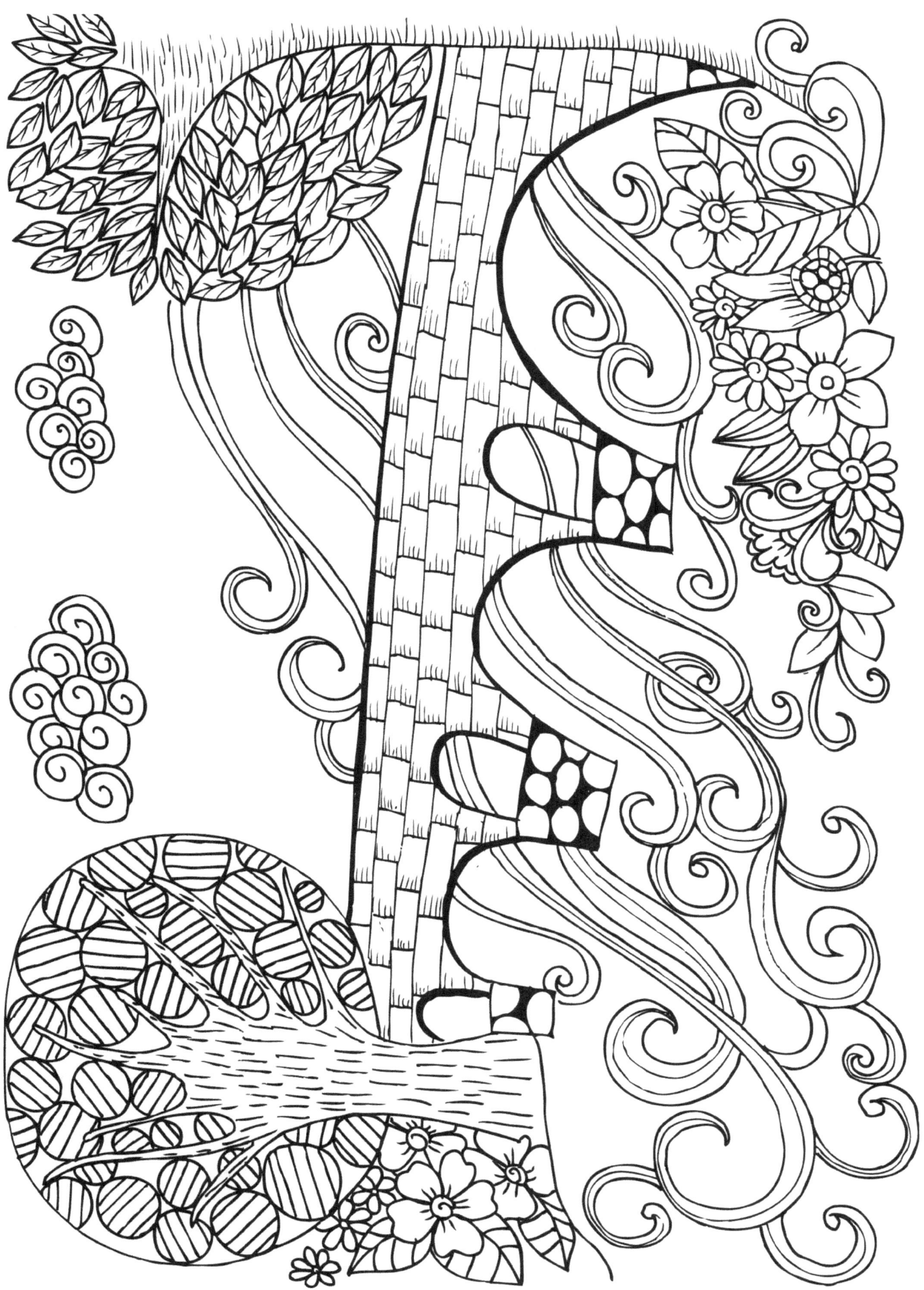

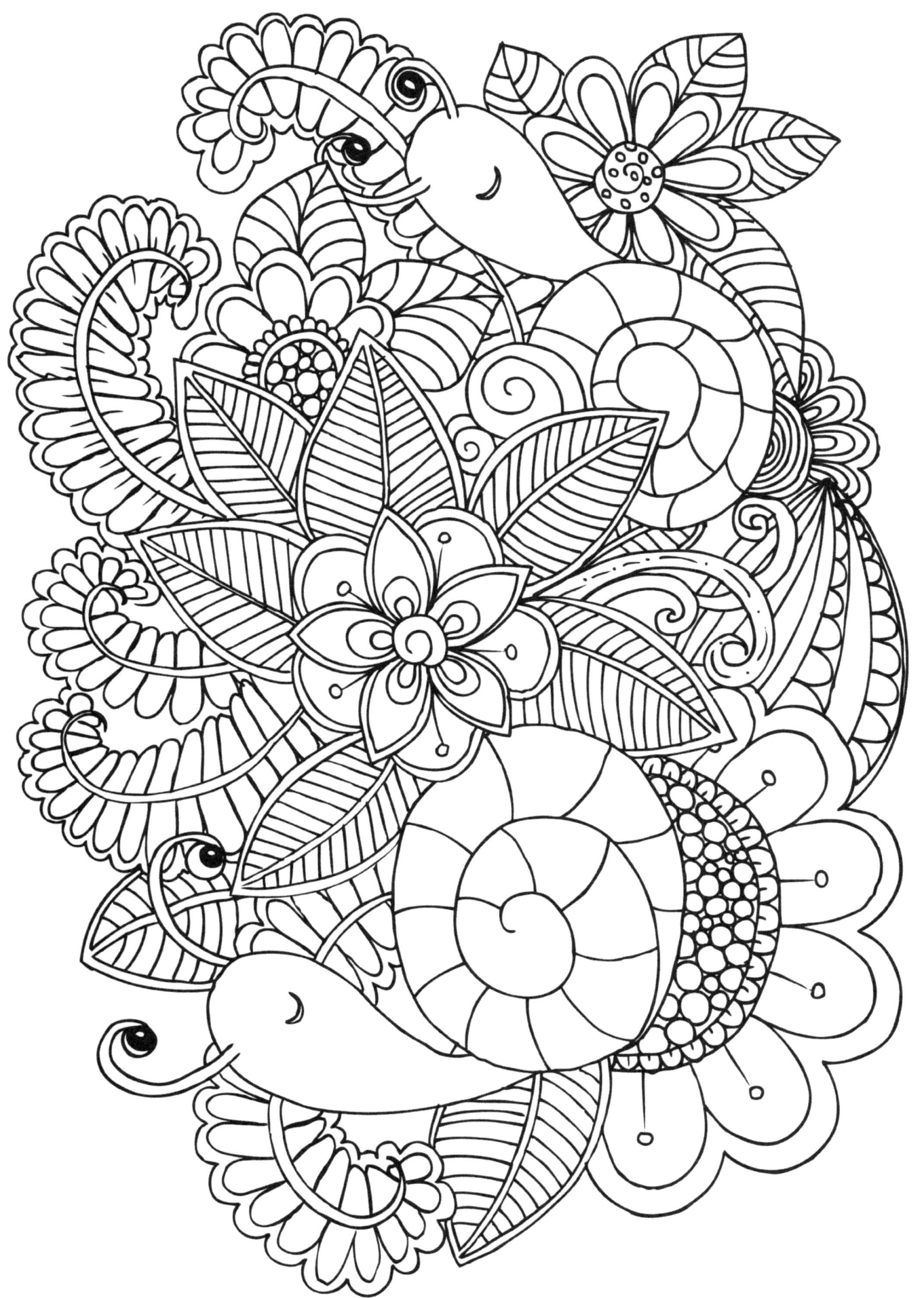

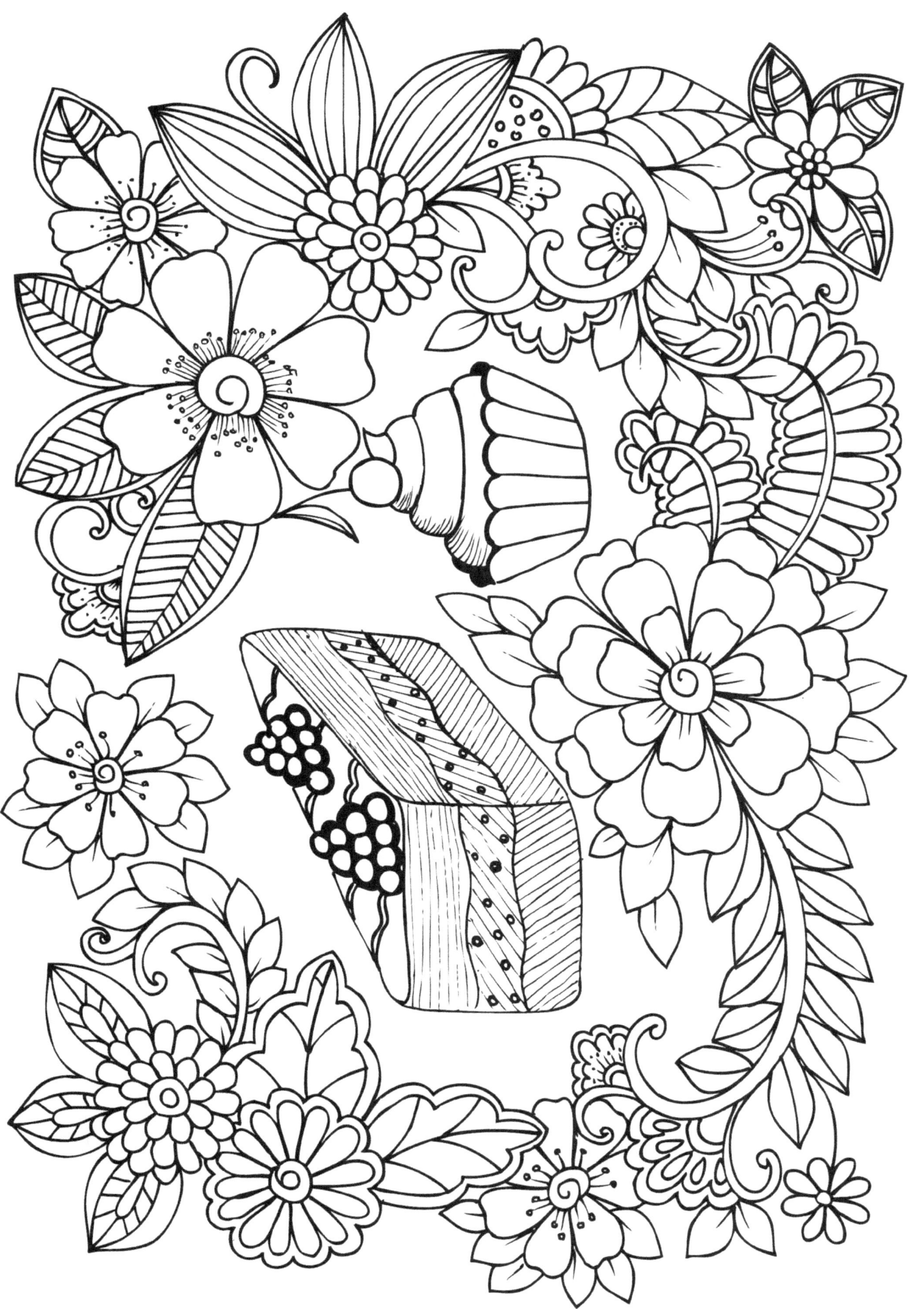

Drawings

Drawings

Best Selling Art Therapy Coloring Books

Coloring Books For Adults:

- Zombie Coloring Book: Black Background
- Butterfly Coloring Book For Adults: Black Background
- Tattoo Coloring Book: Black Background
- Coloring Books for Adults Relaxation: Native American Inspired Designs
- Fishing Coloring Book for Adults: Black Background

Coloring Books For Men:

- Coloring Book for Men: Anti-Stress Designs Vol 1
- Coloring Book For Men: Fishing Designs
- Coloring Book For Men: Tattoo Designs
- Coloring Books for Men: Hunting
- Coloring Book For Men: Biker Designs

Coloring Books For Seniors:

- Coloring Book For Seniors: Nature Designs Vol 1
- Coloring Book For Seniors: Anti-Stress Designs Vol 1
- Coloring Books for Seniors: Relaxing Designs
- Coloring Book For Seniors: Floral Designs Vol 1
- Coloring Book For Seniors: Ocean Designs Vol 1

Coloring Books For Teens and Tweens:

- Coloring Books For Teens: Ocean Designs
- Coloring Books for Teen Girls Vol 1
- Teen Inspirational Coloring Books
- Coloring Book for Teens: Anti-Stress Designs Vol 1
- Tween Coloring Books For Girls: Cute Animals

Coloring Books For Kids:

- Horse Coloring Book For Girls
- Coloring Books For Boys: Sharks
- Coloring Books for Boys: Animal Designs
- Unicorn Coloring Book for Girls
- Detailed Coloring Books For Kids

Art Therapy Coloring Books

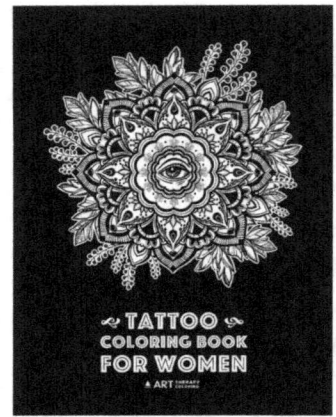

TATTOO COLORING BOOK FOR WOMEN

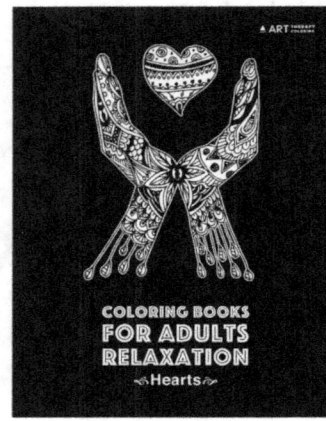

COLORING BOOKS FOR ADULTS RELAXATION
Hearts

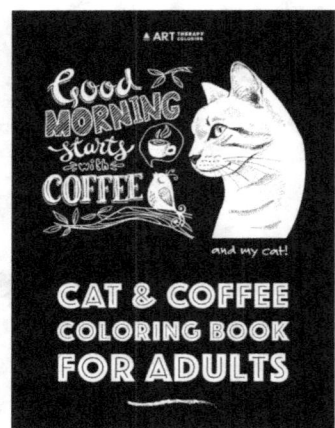

CAT & COFFEE COLORING BOOK FOR ADULTS

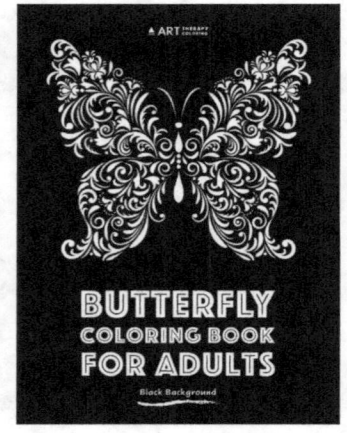

BUTTERFLY COLORING BOOK FOR ADULTS
Black Background

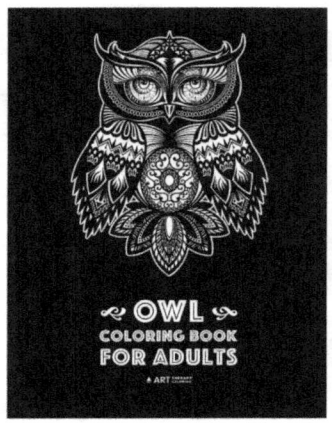

OWL COLORING BOOK FOR ADULTS

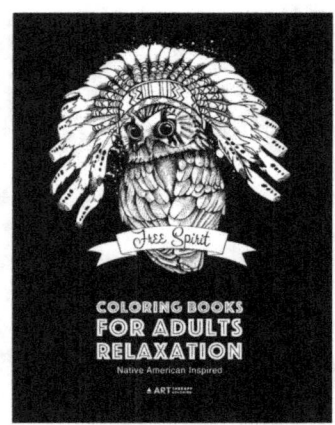

COLORING BOOKS FOR ADULTS RELAXATION
Native American Inspired

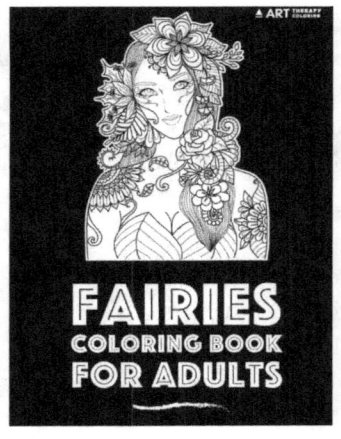

FAIRIES COLORING BOOK FOR ADULTS

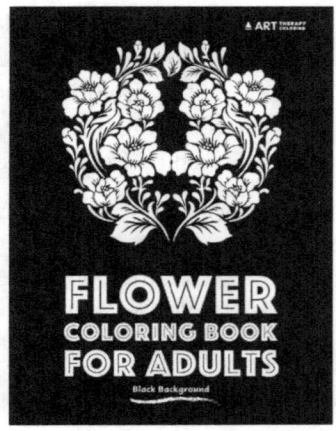

FLOWER COLORING BOOK FOR ADULTS
Black Background

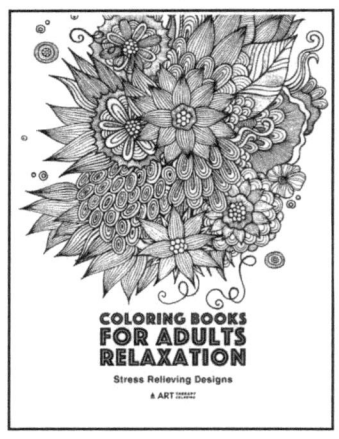

COLORING BOOKS FOR ADULTS RELAXATION
Stress Relieving Designs

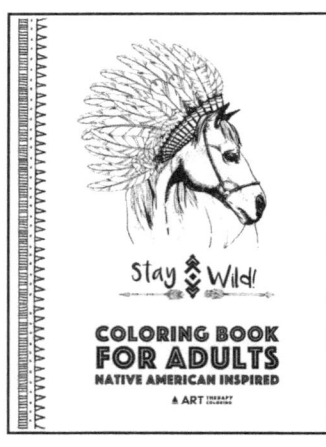

Stay Wild!
COLORING BOOK FOR ADULTS NATIVE AMERICAN INSPIRED

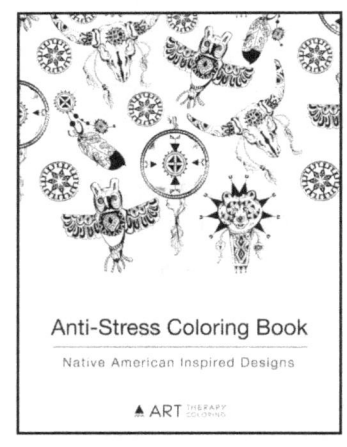

Anti-Stress Coloring Book
Native American Inspired Designs

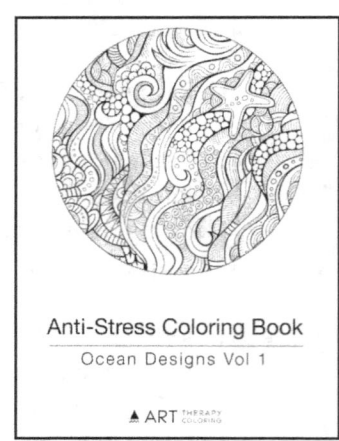

Anti-Stress Coloring Book
Ocean Designs Vol 1

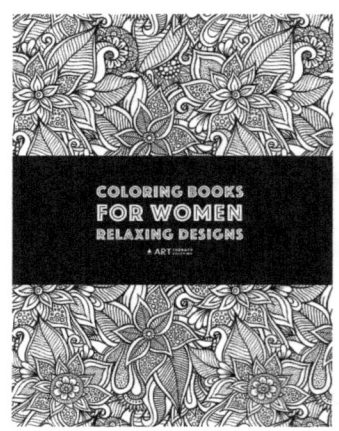

COLORING BOOKS FOR WOMEN RELAXING DESIGNS

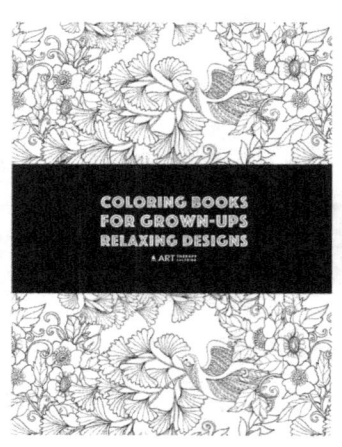

COLORING BOOKS FOR GROWN-UPS RELAXING DESIGNS

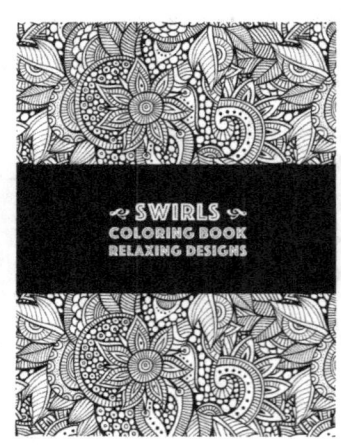

SWIRLS COLORING BOOK RELAXING DESIGNS

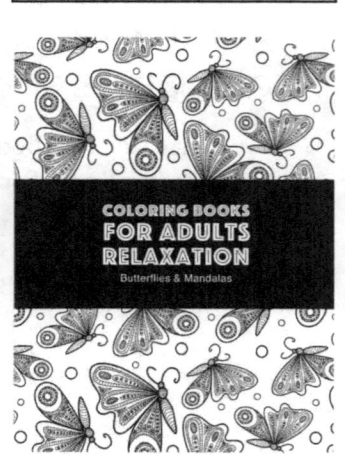

COLORING BOOKS FOR ADULTS RELAXATION
Butterflies & Mandalas

Art Therapy Coloring Books

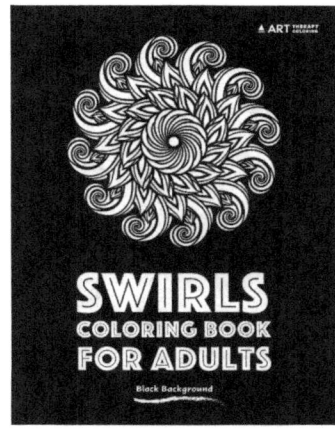
SWIRLS COLORING BOOK FOR ADULTS
Black Background

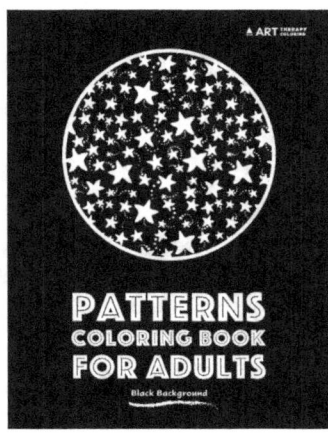
PATTERNS COLORING BOOK FOR ADULTS
Black Background

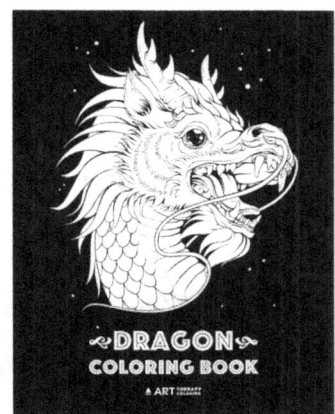
DRAGON COLORING BOOK

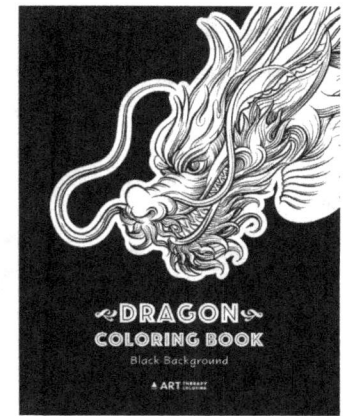
DRAGON COLORING BOOK
Black Background

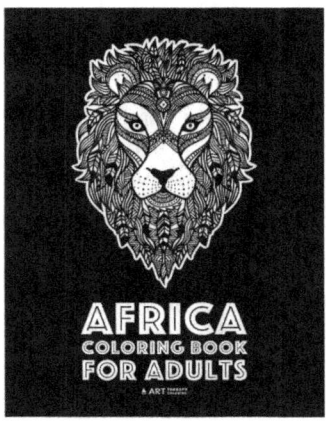
AFRICA COLORING BOOK FOR ADULTS

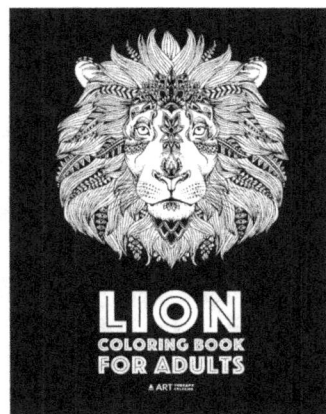
LION COLORING BOOK FOR ADULTS

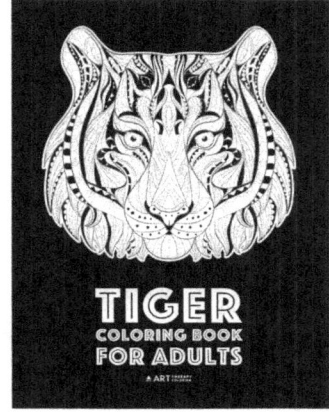
TIGER COLORING BOOK FOR ADULTS

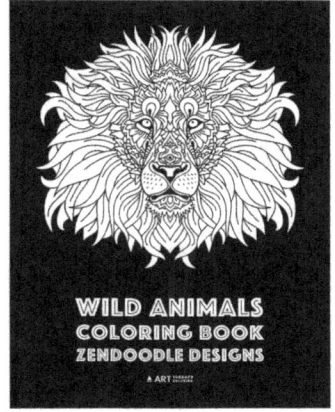
WILD ANIMALS COLORING BOOK ZENDOODLE DESIGNS

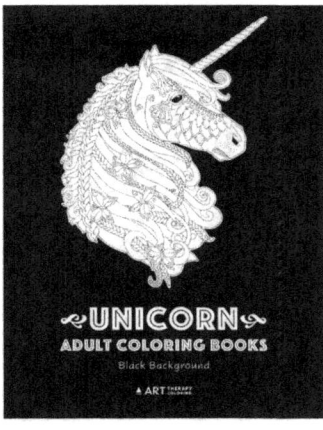
UNICORN ADULT COLORING BOOKS
Black Background

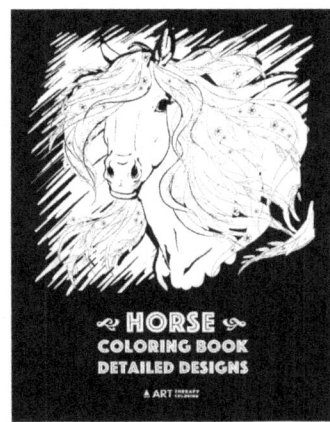
HORSE COLORING BOOK DETAILED DESIGNS

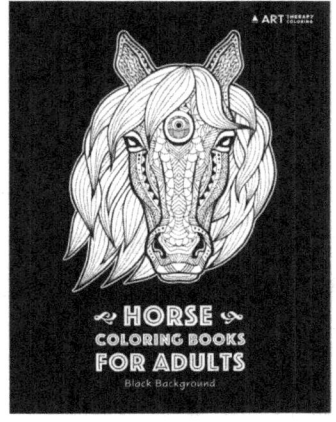
HORSE COLORING BOOKS FOR ADULTS
Black Background

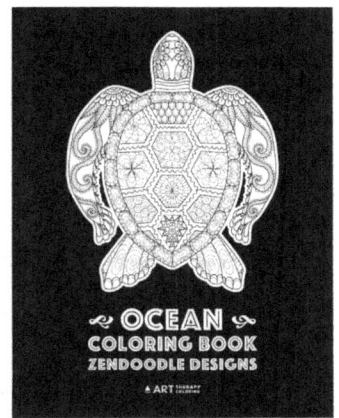
OCEAN COLORING BOOK ZENDOODLE DESIGNS

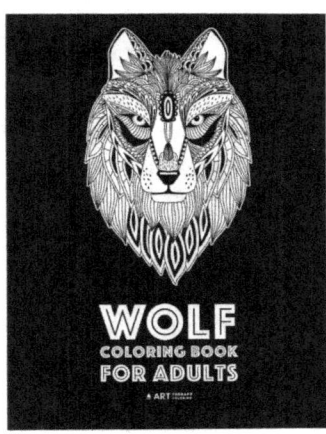
WOLF COLORING BOOK FOR ADULTS

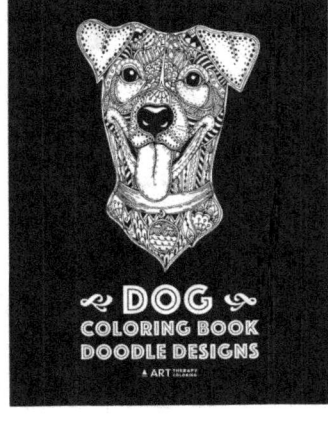
DOG COLORING BOOK DOODLE DESIGNS

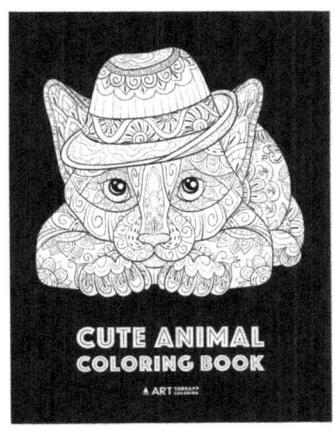
CUTE ANIMAL COLORING BOOK

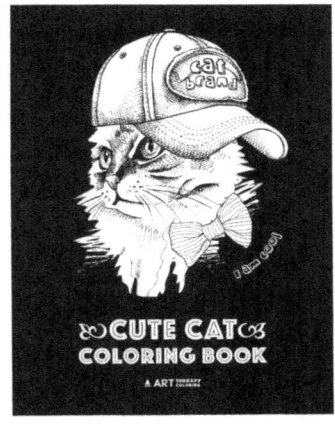
CUTE CAT COLORING BOOK

Art Therapy Coloring Books

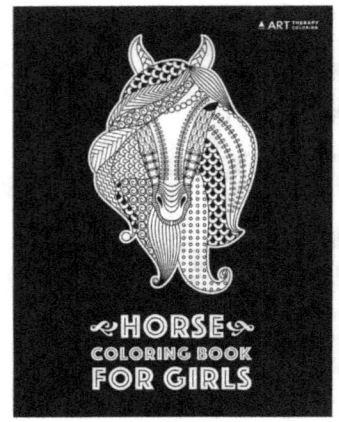

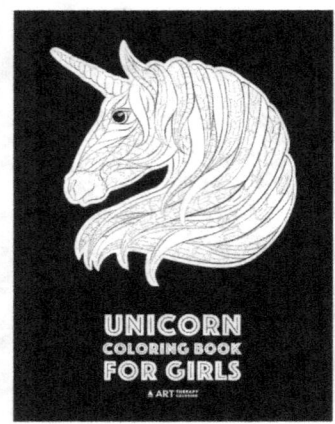

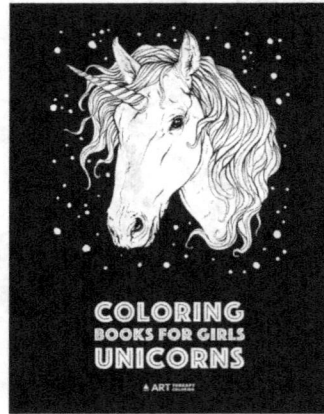

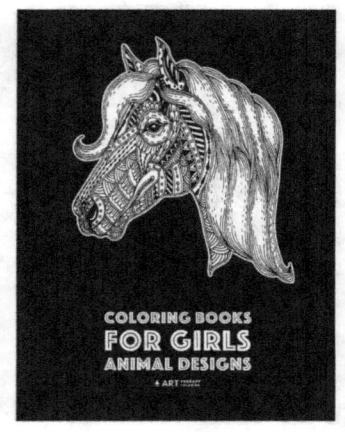

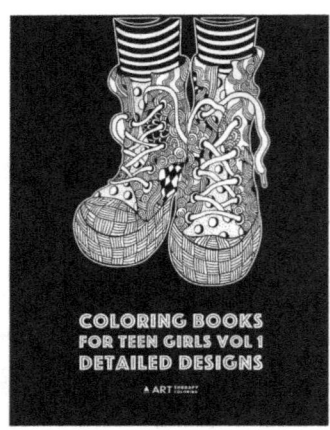

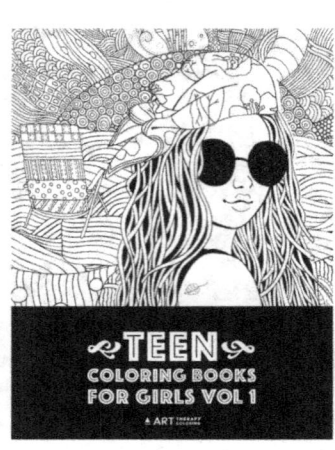

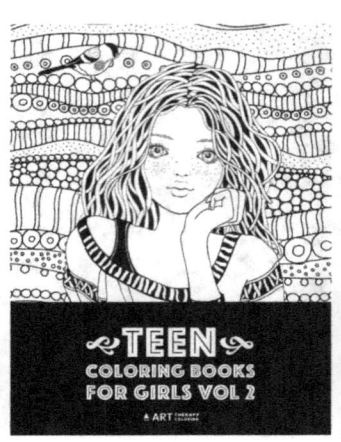

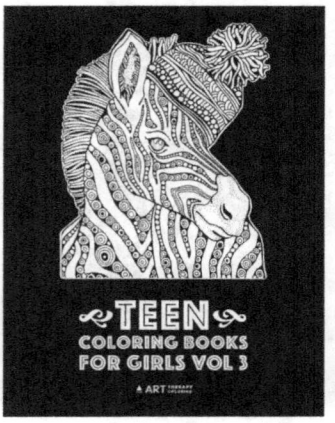

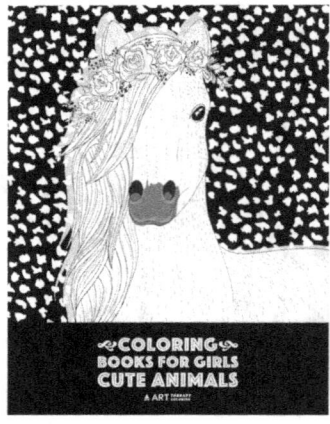

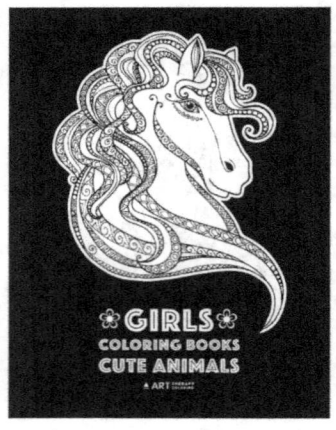

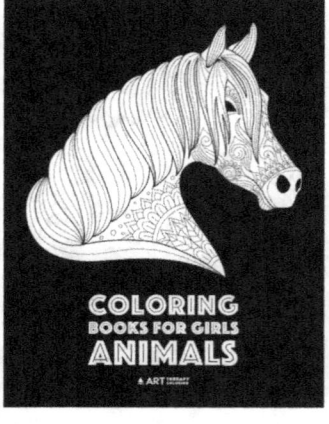

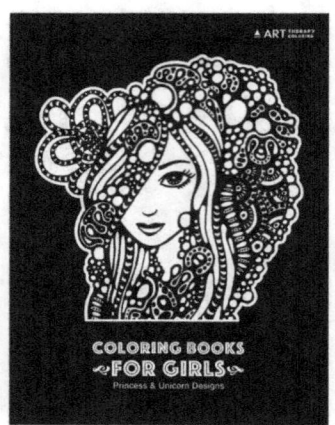

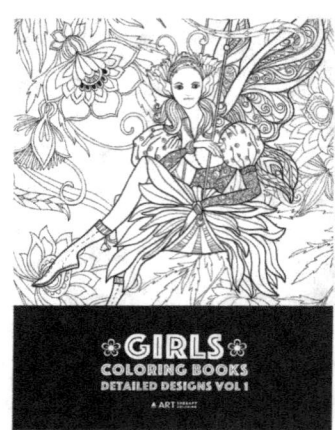

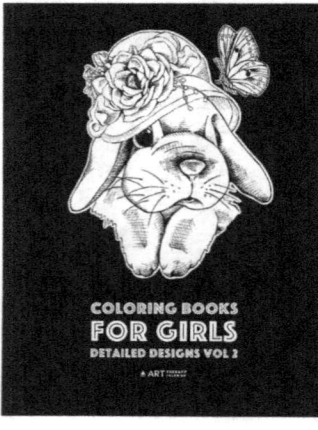

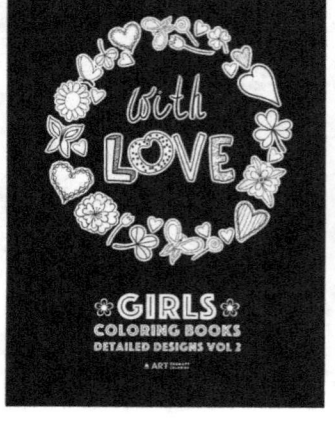

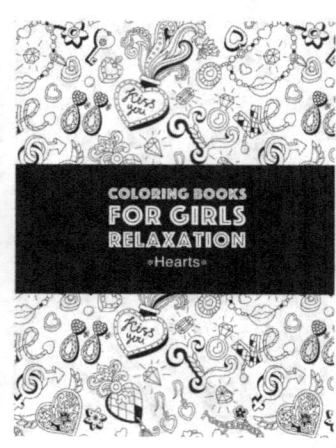

Art Therapy Coloring Books

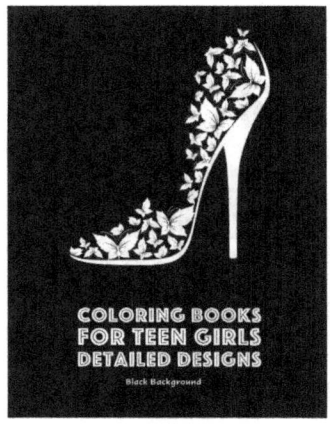

COLORING BOOKS FOR TEEN GIRLS DETAILED DESIGNS
Black Background

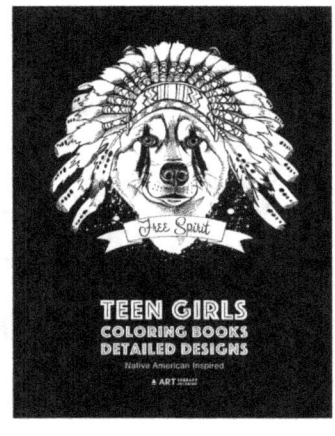

TEEN GIRLS COLORING BOOKS DETAILED DESIGNS
Native American Inspired

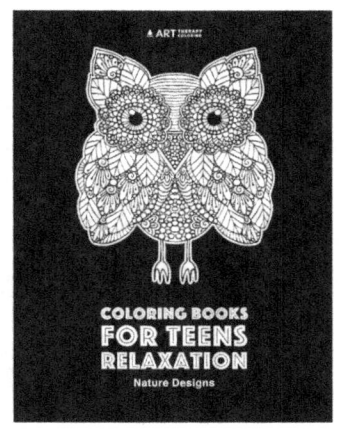

COLORING BOOKS FOR TEENS RELAXATION
Nature Designs

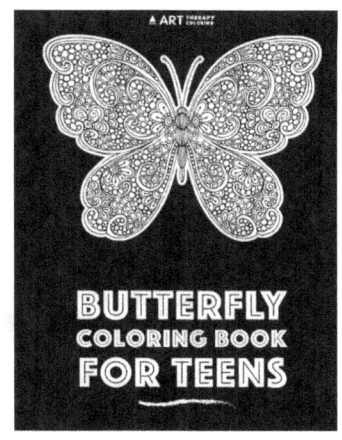

BUTTERFLY COLORING BOOK FOR TEENS

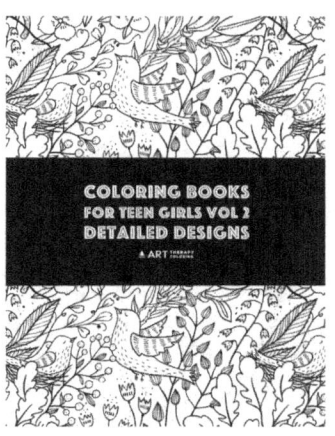

COLORING BOOKS FOR TEEN GIRLS VOL 2 DETAILED DESIGNS

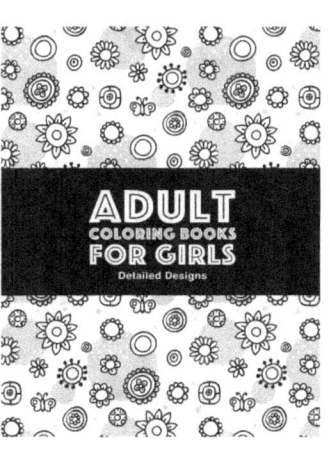

ADULT COLORING BOOKS FOR GIRLS
Detailed Designs

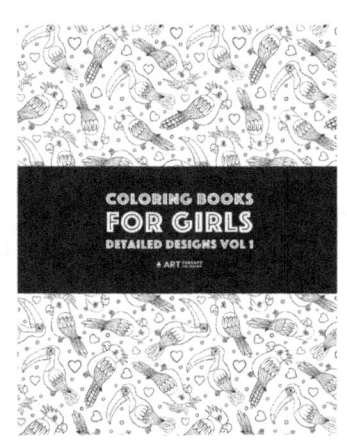

COLORING BOOKS FOR GIRLS DETAILED DESIGNS VOL 1

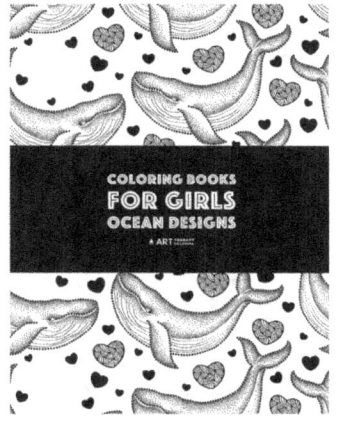

COLORING BOOKS FOR GIRLS OCEAN DESIGNS

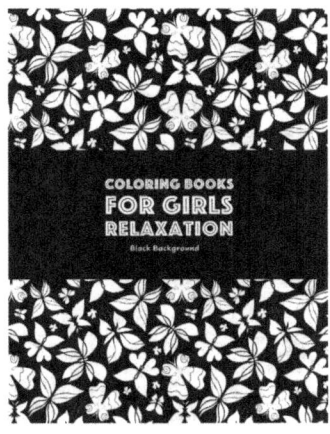

COLORING BOOKS FOR GIRLS RELAXATION
Black Background

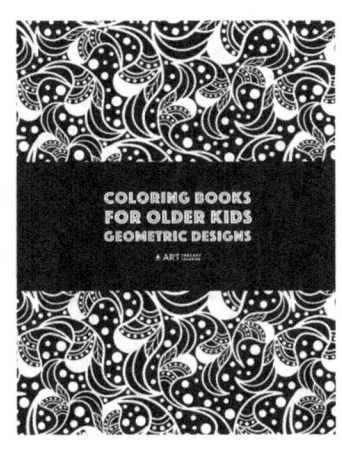

COLORING BOOKS FOR OLDER KIDS GEOMETRIC DESIGNS

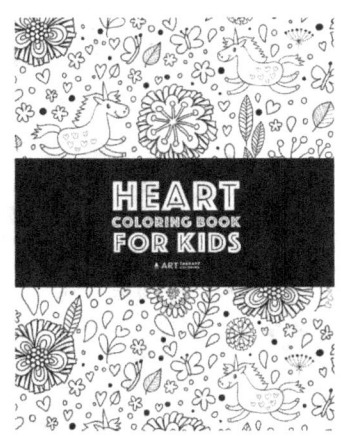

HEART COLORING BOOK FOR KIDS

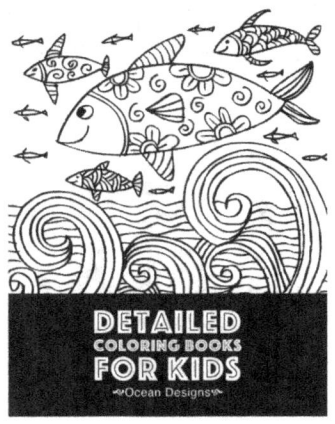

DETAILED COLORING BOOKS FOR KIDS
Ocean Designs

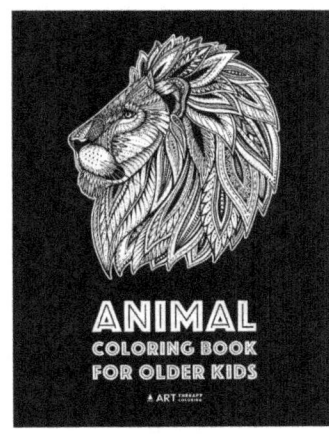

ANIMAL COLORING BOOK FOR OLDER KIDS

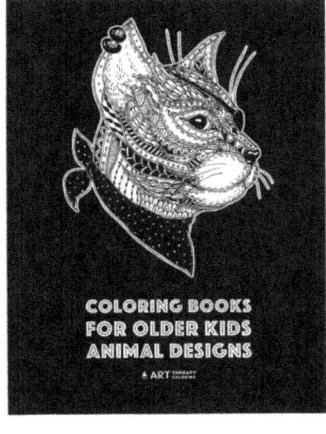

COLORING BOOKS FOR OLDER KIDS ANIMAL DESIGNS

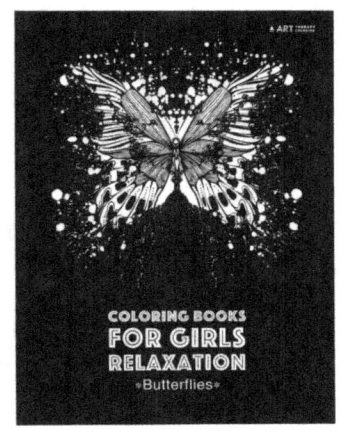

COLORING BOOKS FOR GIRLS RELAXATION
Butterflies

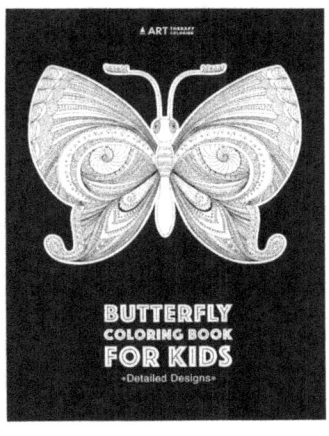

BUTTERFLY COLORING BOOK FOR KIDS
Detailed Designs

Art Therapy Coloring Books

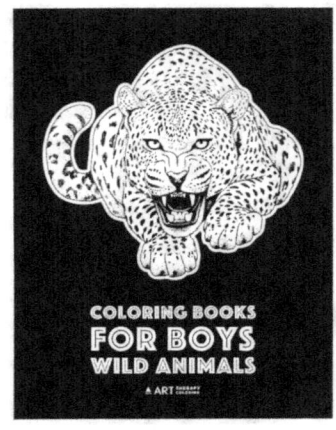

COLORING BOOKS
FOR BOYS
WILD ANIMALS

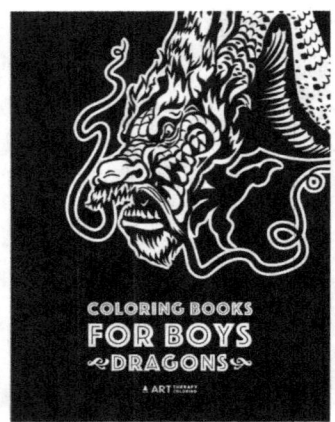

COLORING BOOKS
FOR BOYS
DRAGONS

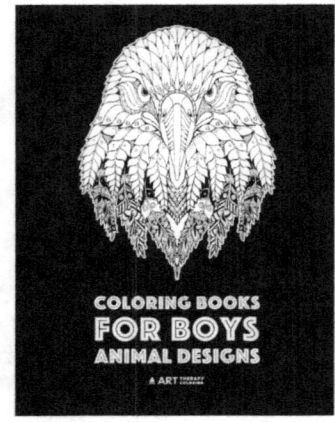

COLORING BOOKS
FOR BOYS
ANIMAL DESIGNS

COLORING BOOKS
FOR BOYS
OCEAN DESIGNS
Black Background

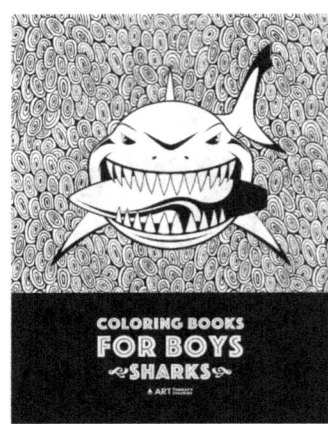

COLORING BOOKS
FOR BOYS
SHARKS

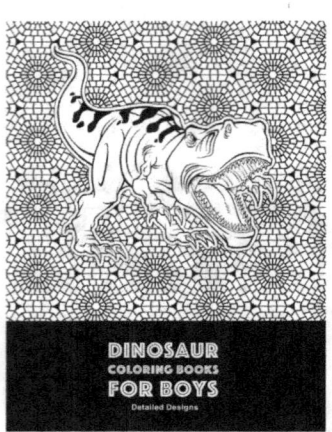

DINOSAUR
COLORING BOOKS
FOR BOYS
Detailed Designs

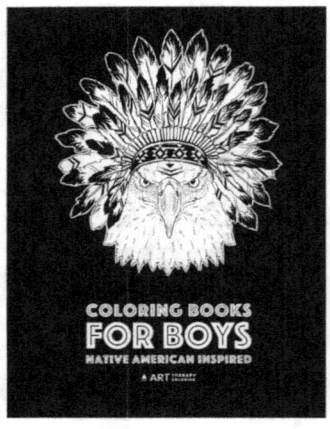

COLORING BOOKS
FOR BOYS
NATIVE AMERICAN INSPIRED

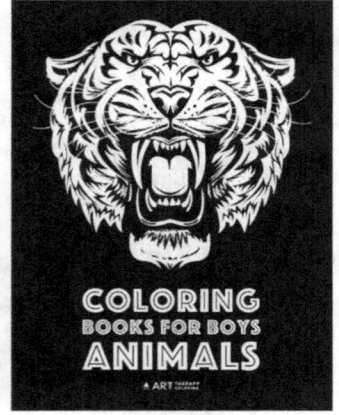

COLORING
BOOKS FOR BOYS
ANIMALS

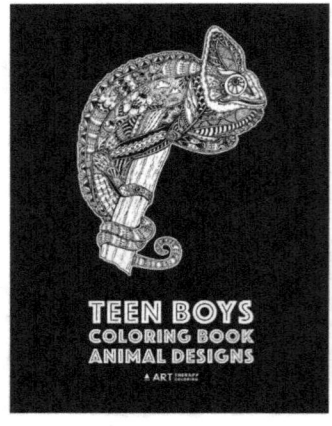

TEEN BOYS
COLORING BOOK
ANIMAL DESIGNS

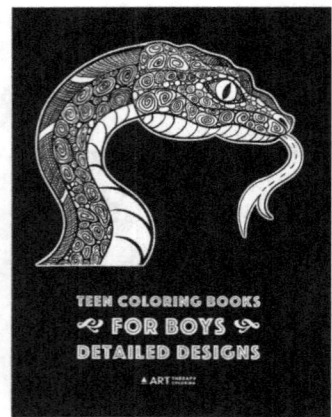

TEEN COLORING BOOKS
FOR BOYS
DETAILED DESIGNS

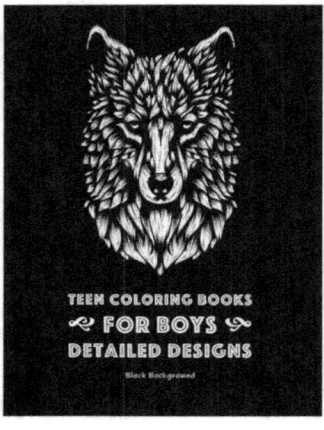

TEEN COLORING BOOKS
FOR BOYS
DETAILED DESIGNS
Black Background

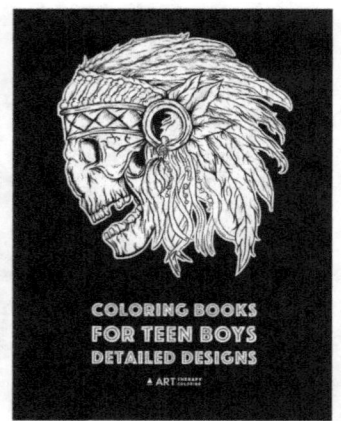

COLORING BOOKS
FOR TEEN BOYS
DETAILED DESIGNS

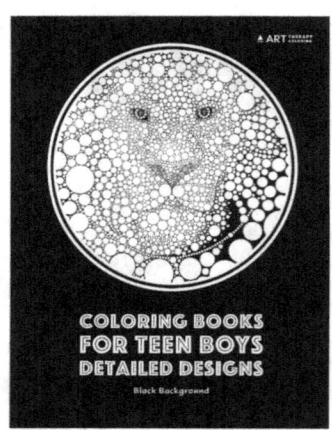

COLORING BOOKS
FOR TEEN BOYS
DETAILED DESIGNS
Black Background

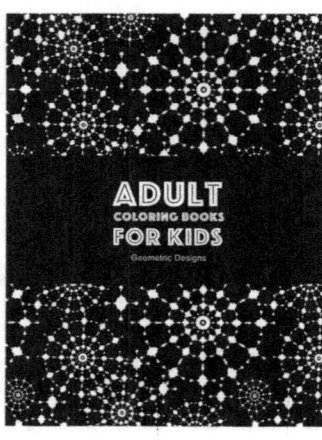

ADULT
COLORING BOOKS
FOR KIDS
Geometric Designs

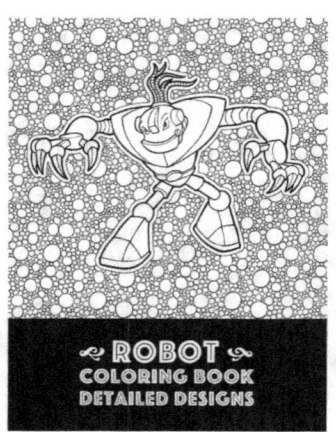

ROBOT
COLORING BOOK
DETAILED DESIGNS

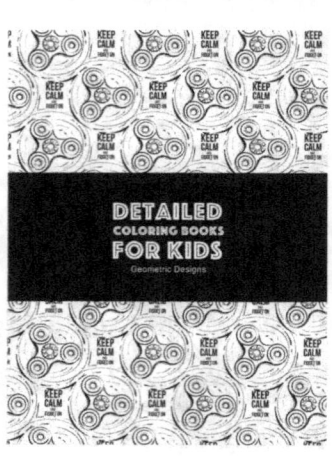

DETAILED
COLORING BOOKS
FOR KIDS
Geometric Designs

Art Therapy Coloring Books

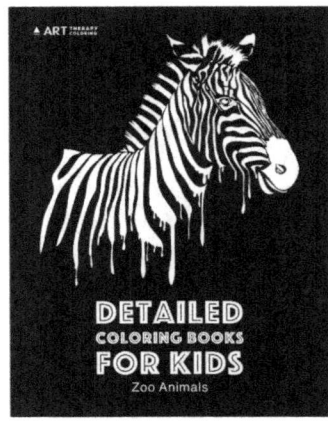

DETAILED
COLORING BOOKS
FOR KIDS
Zoo Animals

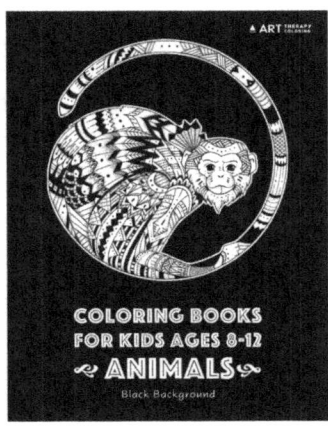

COLORING BOOKS
FOR KIDS AGES 8-12
~ANIMALS~
Black Background

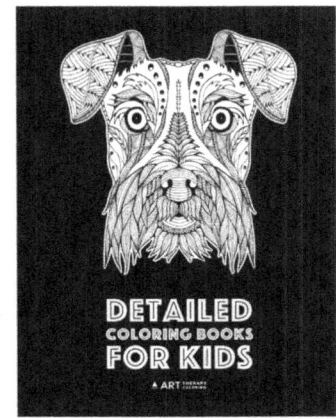

DETAILED
COLORING BOOKS
FOR KIDS

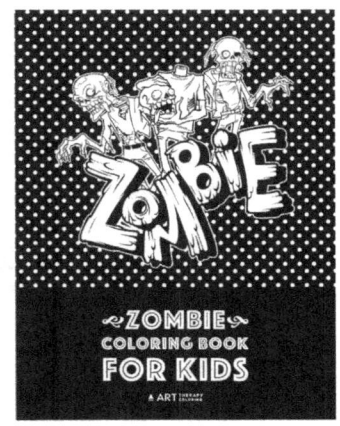

~ZOMBIE~
COLORING BOOK
FOR KIDS

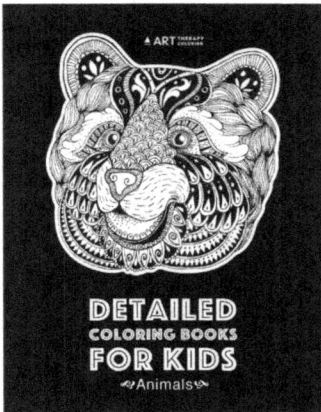

DETAILED
COLORING BOOKS
FOR KIDS
~Animals~

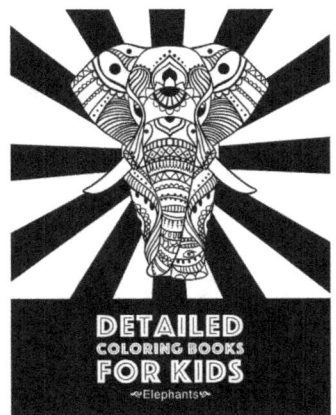

DETAILED
COLORING BOOKS
FOR KIDS
~Elephants~

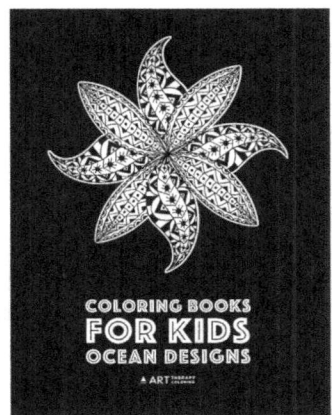

COLORING BOOKS
FOR KIDS
OCEAN DESIGNS

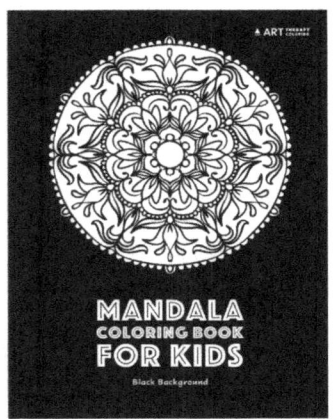

MANDALA
COLORING BOOK
FOR KIDS
Black Background

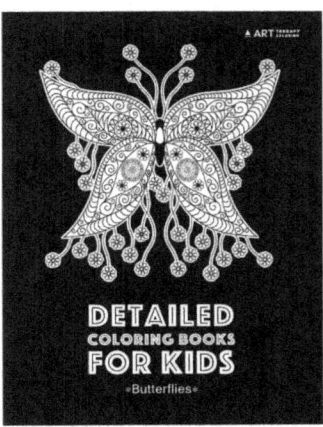

DETAILED
COLORING BOOKS
FOR KIDS
~Butterflies~

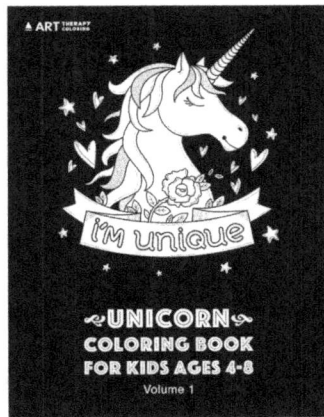

~UNICORN~
COLORING BOOK
FOR KIDS AGES 4-8
Volume 1

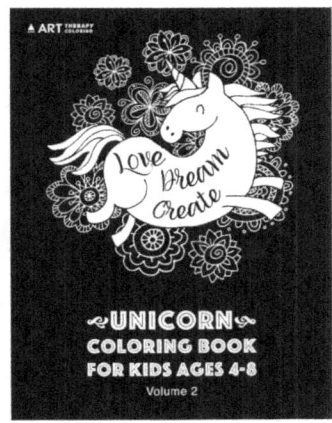

~UNICORN~
COLORING BOOK
FOR KIDS AGES 4-8
Volume 2

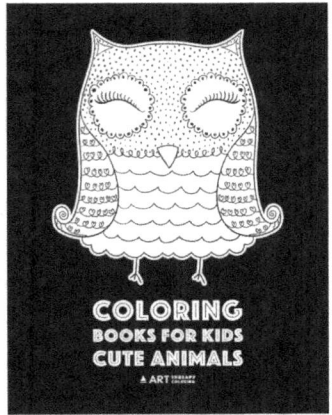

COLORING
BOOKS FOR KIDS
CUTE ANIMALS

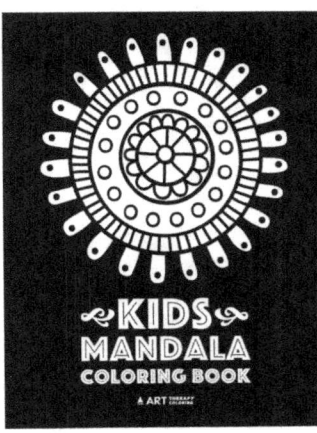

~KIDS~
MANDALA
COLORING BOOK

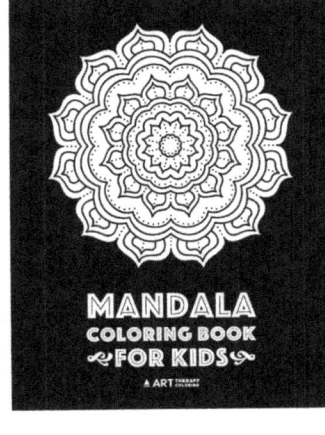

MANDALA
COLORING BOOK
FOR KIDS

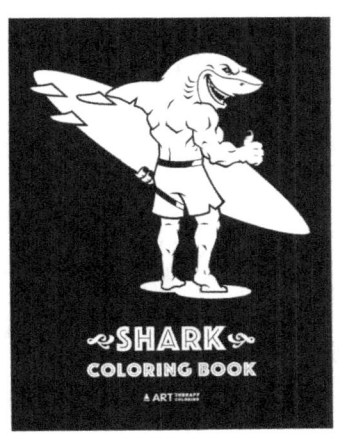

~SHARK~
COLORING BOOK

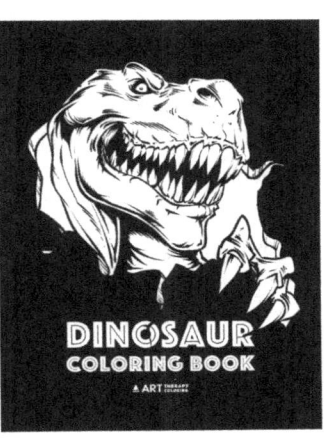

DINOSAUR
COLORING BOOK

Flower Coloring Book
For Adults Vol 5

Published by:
Art Therapy Coloring
www.arttherapycoloring.com

ISBN: 978-1-944427-59-7